❯❯❯·❯❯❯ ✦ ❮❮·❮❮❮

THE NEW MUSIC

1900–1960

❯❯❯·❯❯❯ ✦ ❮❮·❮❮❮

By the same author

✦

WHAT TO LISTEN FOR IN MUSIC
MUSIC AND IMAGINATION
COPLAND ON MUSIC

THE NEW
MUSIC

1900–1960

Revised and Enlarged Edition

❖

AARON COPLAND

W · W · NORTON & COMPANY

New York · London

To Paul Fromm

friend and patron of American composers

W. W. Norton & Company, Inc., 500 Fifth Avenue, New York, N.Y. 10110

W. W. Norton & Company Ltd., 37 Great Russell Street, London WC1B 3NU

ISBN 0-393-00239-X

Contents

⇥⇥✦⇤⇤

2. COMPOSERS IN AMERICA

3. THE PRESENT DAY

Preface

❊❊❊ ✦ ❊❊❊

THE ART OF MUSIC during the present century has undergone a violent upheaval. Audiences everywhere have shown signs of bewilderment at the variety of styles and tendencies that all pass muster under the name of modern music. Being unaware of the separate steps that brought about these innovations, they are naturally at a loss to understand the end result. Speaking generally, the lay listener has remained antagonistic, confused, or merely apathetic to the major creations of the newer composers.

But it has been obvious for some time now, even to the apathetic listener, that the art of music has been passing through a period of revolutionary change. Although this break with the past began more than sixty years ago, there are still some people who have not recovered from the shock. Music has been changing, but they have remained the same. Nevertheless, inwardly, they know that change in music, like change in all the arts, is inevitable. After all, why should I or any other composer living in a time like ours write music that reflects some other period? Isn't it natural for us to try to develop our own kind of music? In doing so, we are merely following the example of revolutionaries like Beethoven and Wagner. They too sought new expressive possibilities in music—and found them.

The fact is that the whole history of music is a history of continuous change. There never was a great composer who left music exactly as he found it. This is true of Bach and Mozart, just as it is true of Debussy and Stravinsky. We can only conclude, therefore, that the period of change through which music has recently passed was, contrary to what many people believe, an inevitable one—part of the great tradition of music throughout the ages.

At any rate, whether we like it or not, music today is radically different from what it was at the start of our century. The purpose of this book is to make the differences more understandable to the lay listener. This is not a textbook, however, in which a detailed and methodical account is given of every phase of new music. It is, rather, a general picture of the highlights of the movement, as it appears to one practicing composer.

The chapters that follow are grouped into three sections: the first follows the course of new music as it gradually emerged in Europe; the second fills out the picture as it was reflected on the North American continent; and the final section examines some of the current trends and preoccupations of the post-1950 generation of composers. By deliberately omitting as much detail as possible from the first two sections, I have tried to clarify the outlines of what might otherwise seem to many a highly involved and often contradictory picture.

In discussing contemporary composers and their styles, or the new musical vocabulary they use, it is naturally impossible to avoid making observations that may also be found in other studies of the same subject. My book offers no brand-new discoveries concerning contemporary music; it attempts only to put into some semblance of order the seemingly opposed and confused tendencies in the music of our time.

Preface to the Revised Edition

⇒≫ ⇒≫ ✦ ≪⇐ ≪⇐

IT IS BOTH an exhilarating and a sobering experience for a composer-author like myself to reread his own book on contemporary music written more than a quarter of a century ago. I feel fortunate to have been able to test past judgments in the light of all that has happened in the field of music since 1941, when *Our New Music* first appeared. For the most part, I am happy to report, I still tend to agree with myself; that is why I have decided to publish a new edition of the book sufficiently revised to bring it up to date.

Here follows a brief account of the changes that have been made:

The change of title from *"Our"* New Music to *"The"* New Music is not meant to imply a subtle disengagement of the author from the musical scene of more recent years. The new title was chosen to indicate that this is not merely a reprint of the original edition. But the reader is cautioned to bear in mind that *Our New Music* was never intended to be a comprehensive review of contemporary music. My purpose, as explained in the Preface of the first edition, was to highlight the main lines of development from late 19th-century to mid-20th-century music, discussing only those composers and tendencies that played a key role in that development. This approach is retained in the revised edition. Thus, although I count myself an admirer of the music of Luigi Dallapiccola and Benjamin Britten and Elliott Carter, the book contains no discussion of their important contributions to present-day music. The same holds true for outstanding younger men whose names and music would have deserved extended treatment in a more complete survey.

What has altered most radically and unpredictably since the book first appeared is the position of the twelve-tone movement. No one could have foreseen the sudden upsurge of interest in dodecaphonic methods on the part of a new postwar generation. This necessitated a rewriting of the account of the Schoenberg School from the perspective of the '60s.

Wherever appropriate, I have added supplementary comment on the work of those composers whose continued production since publication of the book invited further consideration. In my own case I have added several pages to an autobiographical account written in 1939; these continue the story up to the present. This addition has given me the opportunity to clear up certain misconceptions arising from the final pages of the early sketch.

The final three chapters of the original edition were concerned with such matters as the radio, the phonograph, and film music; these discussions are now superannuated and have been removed. In their place is a new third section, which deals with the pre-occupations of the younger men: serialism, aleatory matters, and the new electronic media.

A. C.

Peekskill, N.Y.
1967

Acknowledgments

-》》-》》◆-《《-《《-

THE IDEAS formulated in this book are the residue of articles written and radio talks and lectures given since about 1927. A few of these have been retained here in their original form. The larger part of the book, however, has been entirely rewritten, and much new and hitherto unpublished material has been added.

I wish to thank, first of all, my friend Miss Minna Lederman, editor of *Modern Music,* for allowing me to quote generously from articles originally written for that magazine. For twenty-two years—from 1924 to 1946—Miss Lederman rendered all contemporary composers an invaluable service in astutely editing a magazine that became increasingly essential as a source book for the story of the music of that key period. The chapter devoted to Charles Ives is printed practically in its original form from *Modern Music,* and the sections dealing with jazz influence, Darius Milhaud, and new music in the United States are all based on articles that first appeared there. Without Miss Lederman's kind permission to borrow freely both from my own writings and occasionally from those of others, it is unlikely that this book would have been undertaken.

My thanks are also due to the editors of the *New Republic, Magazine of Art, American Mercury,* and *Twice a Year* for permission to use in whole or in part material that was first printed in their publications.

In 1963 I was invited by my friend Alberto Ginastera, music director of the di Tella Foundation in Buenos Aires, to give a series of six lectures in the Argentine capital on the "Aesthetics of Twentieth Century Music." Some of the new material in the present edition was first prepared for delivery in Spanish on that occasion.

＊≫≫ ✦ ≪≪＊

1. SURVEY OF CONTEMPORARY
EUROPEAN COMPOSERS (1900-1960)

＊≫≫ ✦ ≪≪＊

The Argument

※》》※》 ✦ 《※《※

FEW MUSIC LOVERS realize to what an extent we are dominated in music by the Romantic tradition of the 19th century. A large proportion of the music heard nowadays was created in that century, and most of it came from German-speaking countries. Nothing really new was possible in music until a reaction had set in against that tradition. The entire history of modern music, therefore, may be said to be a history of the gradual pull-away from the Germanic musical tradition of the past century.

The following pages will trace the gathering momentum of this reaction and the different forms it gradually assumed. The first stirrings of a change may easily be traced to Russia. By utilizing their native folk music as a source of inspiration, Russian composers arrived at a totally different result from music based on the art-music tradition of Germany. There is a kind of universality of feeling in a Russian folk tune, quite different from the more intimate quality of German folk music.

Here at its very inception is a basic difference between Romantic and modern music. The German Romantic was highly subjective and personal in the expression of his emotions. The 20th-century composer seeks a more universal ideal. He tends to be more objective and impersonal in his music. The emotional climate of the times has changed. Romanticism, especially in its later stages, now seems overexpressive, bombastic, self-pitying, long-winded. The tempo of modern times calls for a music that is more matter-of-fact, more concise—and, especially, less patently emotional.

I doubt whether the early Russian composers were able to

foresee the far-reaching implications of their new trends. For it was only by very gradual stages that the pull-away from the Germanic tradition was accomplished. It wasn't until the last decade of the 19th century that the anti-German movement found an outspoken leader in France in the person of Claude Debussy. And although he himself never managed to free his style from a kind of passive Romanticism, he nevertheless showed the way to younger men like Ravel and Stravinsky.

This all-important change in the expressive ideal of new music was almost entirely overshadowed at first by a number of startling innovations that were introduced into our musical vocabulary at about the same time. I refer, of course, to those dissonant chords and complex rhythms that are synonymous in many people's minds with modern music. But don't be put off by these new musical elements—they are merely the superficial marks of modern music. They change nothing essential. New music, during the first half of our century, is made up basically of exactly the same elements as older music. Needless to say, it has melody, form, rhythm, and harmony, just as familiar music has. But each of these elements has been extended and enriched. I know that these extensions sometimes make the newer music difficult to comprehend for those who have not heard enough of it. But I can assure you that the purpose of the modern composer is not to confuse or annoy honest music lovers but simply to make use of these new resources that have extended the boundaries of music.

Modern music in a word, is principally the expression in terms of an enriched musical language of a new spirit of objectivity, attuned to our own times. It is the music of the composer of today—in other words—*our* music.

Preliminaries

No ONE can hope to understand the spirit of new music without keeping clearly in mind the distinction between the two great musical traditions of the 18th and 19th centuries respectively. This is difficult even for a professional musician, for we all tend to hear the music of the 18th century with the ears of the 19th. It is not a simple matter to listen to the music of Couperin, Rameau, or Gluck and at the same time completely blot out of one's memory the music of Weber, Schumann, or Liszt. Inevitably our familiarity with the music of the 19th century colors our reactions to the music of the century that preceded it.

Yet these two periods are completely opposed in their musical objectives. The Romantic 19th century, being closer to us, is easier for us to understand—not only because it is closer in time, but also because something was added by the Romantic composers that made music appear to have greater warmth and more humanity than it ever had before. It is as if music acquired a new dimension, as if composers had never before appreciated how deeply expressive music could be. This newly added emotional power has exerted an almost hypnotic effect on music lovers everywhere. In spite of themselves, audiences tend to seek a similar kind of emotional stimulation in the works of all composers—Romantics and pre-Romantics alike.

This plain fact is crucial to our understanding of 20th-century music. For our music, like the music of the 18th century, does not have as its purpose the creation of that type of intense feeling that is generally called romantic. This is far from saying that our music is without any emotional content whatsoever. But both the quality of emotion and the expressive form that it takes have definitely changed. The present-day listener must be prepared to broaden his musical sensibilities; otherwise he will be seeking a kind of emotional outlet that it is not the intention of the modern composer to provide.

We shall, perhaps, be better able to understand the music of our own period if we study more closely the differences in expressive ideals between the so-called Classic composer of the 18th century and the Romantic composer of the 19th century.

It is safe to assume that composers of both schools started from an equivalent fund of emotion. How does it come about, then, that the music that they wrote is so different in the expression of these same emotions? There are, of course, many reasons connected with environment, with the epoch, and with the functional purpose of the music. But in essence, it seems to me that a large part of the difference is attributable to the composers' attitudes toward their work at the moment of creation. Our only way of knowing what those attitudes may have been is to examine the resultant music.

In the work of the Classic composer, the musical creation itself gives every sign of having been conceived in a spirit of objectivity. A certain air of impersonality hovers about the music. There appears to be no undue stressing of the emotional message. To the Classic composer it was apparently axiomatic that musical sounds are, by their very nature, carriers of emotion. No need, therefore, to concentrate on anything but the manipulation of the musical materials, these to be handled with consummate taste and craftsmanlike ability. There could be no question of the conscious projection of the composer's personality into the composition, making that one of its vital elements, for that was the part of creation that could be taken for granted, just as it could be taken for granted that the composer would read, think, sleep, and live in his own individual way. Similarly, he could write music only in his own way—assuming, of course, that he was the possessor of true individuality. All emphasis at the moment of creation, therefore, could be placed upon the beauty of the musical line, the perfection of form, the heavenliness of the music for its own sake or for whatever purpose it was written. Working at his compositions from this viewpoint, the Classic composer could more easily achieve an absolute purity of musical proportion.

The Romantic in music, on the other hand, worked from an entirely different premise. He began with the idea that his music was unique—unique by virtue of the fact that it was primarily an expression of his own personal emotions. This subjective attitude put all emphasis on the open and uninhibited display of personal feelings. And it was because this particular kind of romantic feeling was really new—had never been heard in music before— that the 19th-century composer exerted and, in all probability, will continue to exert his extraordinary hold on the imaginations of music lovers throughout the world.

To the Romantic composer musical sounds in themselves were meaningless. Only insofar as a meaning could be found behind and beyond the notes, so to speak, could music be said to be interesting. At this point a new and important component was made an integral part of music—the psychological factor. Music could now be written not for its own sake alone but for the purpose of inducing psychological reactions in the hearer. For what seemed like the first time, it was discovered that music possesses a magical and evocative power—a poetic content beyond anything dreamed of by the 18th-century composer.

No one would wish to deny that the 19th century added something truly original to the art of music. What the English critic H. C. Colles says, is true: "The Romantic Movement, if it meant anything, meant the deepening of the expressiveness of music. . . ." It is because of that fact, however, that Mr. Colles cannot understand why modern composers should now be saying, to use his own words: "Above all things, we must get away from the baleful influence of the Romantic Movement." "Why?" he asks, rather pitifully. Why, indeed! Because the new vein of expressiveness opened up by Beethoven at the beginning of the century had reached the exhaustion point by the time Wagner died in 1883. It is necessary only to listen to the music of Wagner's successors to be convinced of that. By the turn of the century it was clear that German music, which had led the world for more than a hundred and fifty years, was incapable of renewing itself. It served no purpose longingly to point to the triumphs of a period gone by as an example for a new generation of composers to follow. A fresh start had to be made.

This idea was first understood by composers outside Germany, as was natural. To disengage music from its Romantic roots was no easy undertaking. Fortunately for the composers involved, artistic creation need never know too consciously where it is leading. It was only very gradually that music moved out of the sphere of the Romantic era and eventually found itself following ideals incorporated in the music of the 18th century.

There is, of course, no question of writing music today that might be mistaken for music composed in the 18th century. That would be mere pastiche and lead to artistic suicide. But what we shall find in detail later in this book is that composers of today write their music from a premise that has definite resemblance to the Classic composer's premise. It goes without saying that some of today's music displays certain Romantic traits. But, speaking generally, the typical contemporary composer prefers an objective, impersonal approach; a complex, contrapuntal texture; a concentration on perfection of line and beauty of proportion.

Now let us see from what remote beginnings this end result was finally arrived at.

The Background—Late Nineteenth Century

‐⫸‐⫸ ✦ ⫷‐⫷‐

Nationalism

IN LINE WITH its melodramatic nature, German Romanticism contained the germ of its own destruction. This bacillus spread to many countries under the name of nationalism.

The international aspect of 18th-century music has often been pointed out. Constant Lambert, the English composer, once wrote that ". . . for the most part eighteenth century composers chose to address their audiences in a cultivated Esperanto with its roots in Italian." This is an amusing way of saying that the Classic composer wrote in a Pan-European style, a style in which the composer no more felt the need of stressing his country of origin than he felt impelled to stress his own individual personality.

It was the Romantic movement that first discovered the special charm of music that evokes a particular landscape. The example set by Weber in his opera *Der Freischütz,* based on local German folklore and making use of popular melodies, let loose a whole Pandora's box of nationalisms. What could be more natural? Each country that possessed a folklore of its own and, as corollary, a folk music of its own had every reason to exploit the local atmosphere. One small country after another added its distinctive voice to the chorus of musical nations. At first there was Gade in Denmark, Grieg in Norway, Smetana in Bohemia. Much later Hungary, Finland, Spain, Poland, and a dozen others joined in.

This new note—an offshoot of Romanticism's interest in the natural, democratic man—seemed to supply a host of European composers with an easy key to musical independence. In most cases this was an illusion. We can see now that the occasional introduction of musical materials—rhythmic, melodic, or harmonic—that stressed local color was not by itself sufficient to free music from the clichés of German musical procedure. There are numbers of symphonies based on national melodies that are hopelessly German in every other respect. The way out was found by those few composers who, taking their native songs as the basis for their work, were able to construct a music on formal and emotional lines independent of the German tradition. This meant the abandonment of most of the structural refinements of Western music: sonata form, fugal treatments, development sections, and so forth. It meant, furthermore, the setting up of new criteria for the judgment of music that existed outside the realm of the standardized German product.

It was the Russians of the last century who first developed a whole school of composers imbued with this idea. In the Russian musical scene of the second half of the 19th century we see enacted the fundamental drama of nationalism in music: the impact of a strongly established Western musical culture with its own art forms upon an equally strong native, but unformed, musical consciousness. The instigator of Russian musical independence was, of course, Glinka. But the role he played in starting the nationalist school seems to have been largely an unconscious one. Glinka began with no thought of breaking down traditions of formal structure. All he tried for was the occasional introduction of a bit of local color. That is why the unusual exoticisms in the choral writing of his operas exist side by side with the familiar Italianate style of the arias. Nevertheless, the national note was sufficiently strong for the younger composers to draw the proper conclusions.

The story of the young group of talented dilettantes who were inspired by Glinka's example has something of the elements of a Russian fairy tale. With very little outside encouragement, and mainly through their own efforts, they tried to learn first the basic principles governing their art and then the way to use these principles so that they should produce a typically Russian music. As M. D. Calvocoressi puts it: "Suddenly launched in the midst of things, they had to make their own bricks (and even learn the technique of brick-making) as well as to discover the architectural principles of which they stood in need. Considering the formidable difficulties in their way, the wonder is, not that they failed to do better, but that they achieved as much as they did."

The dangers of dilettantism are real enough, as we can see from the weaknesses of the Russian school, which are becoming more and more apparent. Rimsky-Korsakov, aware of his lack of a firm grounding, went to the other extreme and lost much of his freshness through too great a fondness for academic formulas. Balakirev and Borodin wrote comparatively little, and much of their work is repetitious. Even so, their music provided a pleasant relief from the philosophical ponderousness of the Germans. What they wrote has, instead, the colorful, storybook quality of music steeped in the legends and landscapes of their own country.

Nowadays it is generally agreed that only one member of the "famous handful" was able to write a music entirely free from the conventions of the German tradition—the composer of the operatic masterpiece *Boris Godunov*.

Mussorgsky's Realism

MODEST MUSSORGSKY, creator of *Boris* and most important member of the Russian Five, is the archetype of the pioneer in music. Living in an atmosphere saturated with Italian and German music, he nevertheless was able to extricate himself from the conventions and prejudices of the time. He had one all-pervading desire for his music: he wished above all things that it be real, that it be natural and simple.

It is difficult to decide to what degree his amateur status in music enabled him to carry out this aim. The blunt statement that Mussorgsky was an amateur composer is, of course, a gross exaggeration. But at the same time it is hard to imagine how he might have conceived his unusual harmonies and forms if he had been put through the German conservatory mill. His entire mature output was distinguished by the fact that it was different from the music being written in his time. His work represents the first really successful attempt to pull music away from the German tradition.

Mussorgsky's music takes its being directly from folksong. This is most striking in his melodies, which are often interchangeable with true peasant songs. They employ typical intervallic changes that completely remove them from the orbit of Occidental music. As has already been stated, there is a kind of universality of feeling in a Russian folk tune. Mussorgsky's melodies retain all the flavor of the originals, and if anything, intensify that profoundly human quality of the Slavic folk expression.

Rhythmically also, Mussorgsky's music derived from Russian folksong. His rhythms have the naturalness of a spoken line, with all the subtle variety of prose speech. By comparison, German music of the same period is unimaginative, tending to stress each accented beat at regular intervals, like a schoolboy's scanning of verses. In Mussorgsky's music we find the germ of many of those later rhythmic developments that have so profoundly influenced all new music. The rhythmic freedom to be found in Stravinsky's early works, and thereafter in the works of a whole generation of modern composers, is directly attributable to the innovations of Mussorgsky and his fellow Russians.

Mussorgsky was much more venturesome than his colleagues in his use of harmony. At times the harmonic skeleton is suggestive of the modal characteristics of the music of the Greek Catholic church, but at others Mussorgsky's harmonies could only have sprung full-blown out of his own daring imagination. (The well-known "corrections" by Rimsky-Korsakov of many of Mussorgsky's compositions have only served to enhance our sense of the boldness of the original versions.) Fundamentally, Mussorgsky's harmonic practice brought into question all those established rules of harmonic procedure that had served composers since Rameau's day. It was a matter not of gradually undermining those rules through the broadest possible interpretation, as Wagner did, but of starting from the premise that the sole judge of good and evil, harmonically speaking, must always be the composer's musical instinct. Here again the harmonic freedom of present-day composers is traceable, in part, to the daring of Mussorgsky.

More important than any of these technical innovations, however, was the spirit animating the notes themselves. One can find harmonic originality in Chopin or Liszt, unconventionalities of rhythm in Berlioz or Schumann, melodic invention in Wagner —but these men were all Romantics. Mussorgsky was a realist in music. He wished above all to be true to nature—true to his own nature and to the humanity about him. In all his work—songs, piano pieces, or operas—there is evidence of a surpassing dramatic gift that informed everything he touched with meaning. But he dramatized not himself or his own private emotions, but those of whatever subject he had in hand. This is what gives his music the impersonal aspect that eventually was to guide all music out of the Romantic impasse. His emotions were objectivized so that they were expressed through the character of Boris, or of the painter Hartmann's pictures, or the many nursery scenes he so fondly depicted.

There is a wonderful rightness about all this music. But even more essential to our immediate purpose is the fact that despite the completely individual nature of his style—and no composer was more personal than Mussorgsky—it is always used for "impersonal" ends, as if Mussorgsky felt that he was important to us only insofar as he was able to make real and universalize the so typical humanity of his Russian characters. That is the meaning of realism in music. Mussorgsky's reality was not that of his own subjective inner world, but that of the world around him, which, using him as a sensitive musical agent, translated itself into living musical terms.

It is this ability to objectify one's emotional reactions that we shall find more and more evident in the work of the newer composers.

The Impressionism of Debussy

WHEN Mussorgsky died in 1881, Claude Debussy was a young man of eighteen, a student in Guiraud's class at the Paris Conservatory. It is one of the curiosities of musical history that Debussy should have found his way to Russia during the following summer as music tutor in the household of the famous Moscow patron of the arts Madame von Meck. It is difficult to determine how much, if any, of the music of Mussorgsky the young musician actually heard or saw during his summer's sojourn. His biographers seem to think none. Nevertheless, it is reasonable to suppose that a young man as talented as Claude Debussy, with eyes and ears open, must have carried away from his Russian visit some conception of music different from that created in the Teutonic image.

This is important, for the dominant figure of the age, in France as elsewhere, was Richard Wagner. Like many other bright young men of the time, Debussy began by becoming an ardent Wagnerite. The influence of that first great enthusiasm reached even as far as *Pelléas*. But at some point during his early career Debussy underwent a change of heart, realizing that the overpowering genius of Bayreuth might prove deadly not only to his own music but to that of all France. From that moment on was born the first conscious will to move music out of the German sphere of influence. In Mussorgsky, the anti-Romantic implication of the music was hardly calculated. It grew more or less naturally out of the nature of the music itself. But in Debussy we have the first example of a composer who openly shouted, "Down with Wagner," and who willingly accepted leadership of the anti-Wagnerian forces.

It is one thing to will the escape from an influence as strong as Wagner's and quite another actually to succeed in carrying it out. That Debussy was helped in freeing himself from the taint of

Wagnerism by Mussorgsky's musical example is obvious to any-one who examines the scores of both composers. Whenever Debussy may have first become acquainted with Mussorgsky's music, in later years he did not hesitate frankly to admit his debt to that Russian master. To his friend Jean-Aubry, on the way to a performance of Mussorgsky's opera, Debussy is reported to have said: "You are going to hear *Boris?* Then you will hear the whole of *Pelléas.*" In both operas the type of musical declamation is the same; the use of modal harmonies and the general economy in the depiction of highly dramatic episodes is also strikingly similar. For in spite of the very considerable contrast in their tempera-ments as artists, the two men had the same regard for poetic truth, the same desire to be simple and real, and the same disdain for all academic solutions.

What belongs to Debussy alone is, of course, his Impressionist aesthetic. Most writers are agreed that here the influence of Symbolist poetry and Impressionist painting was paramount. It was characteristic of the 19th century that painting, literature, and the other arts should have affected musical trends, and the other way about. The poetry of Mallarmé and the painting of Manet gave Debussy more than a hint as to the direction French music ought to take. His own sensitivity as an artist did the rest.

Despite Debussy's awareness of the need for music to take an anti-Romantic turn, it can hardly be said that Impressionism is devoid of Romantic overtones. What Debussy gives us in his music is an exquisite transcription of an ideal world of sensations. Since his music deals with sensations, and since these are often of a passive, hypersensitive, and curiously feminine nature, we are still in the realm of feeling as it was understood and reflected by the Romantic artist. The difference is one of degree rather than of kind. The German Romantic displayed his feelings unabashed. The mounting passion, the explosive climaxes, the sudden changes in dynamic contrast were all quite foreign to Debussy's temperament. Does this mean that the French composer is any the less emotional in his music? Not at all. But the expression that the emotion takes is infinitely more discreet. Debussy's is the

Romanticism of an introvert. All the emphasis and bombast are gone—we move instead in a sentient world of half-shadows, of semithoughts and evanescences. Innumerable commentators have tried to describe the quality of Debussy's art, yet no music ever written more nearly defies description.

If, from an aesthetic standpoint, Impressionism was merely an appendage to the Romantic movement and therefore no "way out" for later composers, the technical innovations introduced by Debussy were far-reaching in their influence.

Most striking to his first listeners was his harmonic originality. Much was written, especially in the beginning, about his harmonic archaisms, about the unheard-of chordal progressions, and, of course, about his substitution of the whole-tone for the ordinary diatonic scale. More important, perhaps, than any of these, but less commented upon at first, was his peculiar use of chord combinations for their purely coloristic value. All these, however, are details in a more profound revolution: the complete breakdown of that system of harmony that had been gradually giving way to the inroads of chromaticism throughout the 19th century and that could now no longer withstand contact with a completely untrammeled harmonic imagination. In essence what Debussy did was simple enough: even more truly than Mussorgsky, he dared to make his ear the sole judge of what was good harmonically. He was able to do this because he was one of the most instinctive musicians who ever lived. What he began, others continued. His work incited a whole generation of composers to experiment with new and untried harmonic possibilities, thereby adding immeasurably to our harmonic resources.

No less original was Debussy's refusal to construct his music along academic lines. It was flying in the face of a century-old tradition to throw overboard all semblance of the clear statement of themes, their subsequent development, and final recapitulation—particularly since Debussy did not establish any system of construction to take the place of the one he discarded. Here again it was his instinct that he trusted. His own music is put together in a highly personal and, on the whole, satisfactory way. Since his time, form in music has tended toward greater and greater freedom—at least, until the reaction brought on in recent years by the return to 18th-century models. One might conservatively predict that composers in the future will again turn to a study of Debussy's form in order to continue the discoveries he made toward a more subtle joining together of musical materials.

The essence of his life's work is to be found in the twenty-four piano Preludes, the best of the songs, the orchestral Nocturnes, and *Pelléas and Mélisande*. In recent times these compositions have been accepted wholeheartedly by the "big" public. Now we are beginning to judge them as the future must judge them, forgetting their revolutionary associations and thinking of them solely as music. This is not easy to do. They possess a fragrance and a delicacy that does not bear too close scrutiny.

Someone once remarked that there is a little bit of Massenet in every Frenchman. I am afraid that Debussy is no exception to that bon mot. It is his sentimental side that is already wearing thin in many of the lesser works. Despite his musical iconoclasm, Debussy was the hedonistic poet of a thoroughly bourgeois world. There is something cushioned and protected, something velvety-soft and overcomfortable about his music. It reflects a span of life when Europe thought itself most secure, between the years 1870 and 1914. One wonders what the eventual fate of this music will be in the uncertain world ahead. A time may come when it will seem overrefined, decadent, effeminate. But no world that we can foresee would ever wish to do without Debussy's music when he is at his best. At such times he is matchlessly poetic and touching and sensitive. All portents would seem to indicate that it will be a long time before French music produces another musician with the soul of a Debussy.

The Late Romantics: Mahler, Strauss, Scriabin, Fauré, Sibelius

OUR STORY OF the gradual emergence of present-day music would be incomplete without a backward glance at some important figures in the musically creative world of 1910. These men were Romantics certainly—they wrote their music in the tradition of Chopin or Wagner or Schubert or Tchaikovsky—yet younger men were able to borrow something technically important from their work. The music of these late Romantics faced two ways: aesthetically it added little, since it attached itself to a tradition that had already fulfilled its promise, but the technical means employed—the harmonies, the contrapuntal textures, the orchestral timbres, the melodic lines—contained elements that were capable of being disengaged and used for new ends. As composers, the Austrian Gustav Mahler, the German Richard Strauss, the Russian Alexander Scriabin, the Frenchman Gabriel Fauré, and the Finn Jean Sibelius had little in common except for their Romantic bias and the forward-looking element, different in each case, of their music. It is well to remember that the quality of their music is not necessarily impaired because it had only a technical influence. Each one of these composers had something of his own to contribute, even though they all belong to the post-Romantic world.

Of these five men I should say that Mahler had most to give to the music of the future. This, no doubt, seems paradoxical, since he was more frankly the Romantic than any of the others. In fact, his greatest work, *The Song of the Earth,* is in many respects the swan song of the entire Romantic movement. There is something symbolic in the reluctance of the composer to touch the final chord in the concluding movements of both this work and his Ninth Symphony. It is as if the composer knew, deep down inside himself, that he was saying a final farewell to the 19th century. All his music reinvokes the past glories of that golden age, but with an added note of regret for a wonderful epoch that is gone without hope of recall.

It is impossible to understand the music of Mahler without keeping in mind that he was by nature a profoundly childlike artist, yet heir to all the problematical complexities of the modern world. The special poetry of his music comes from this naïveté, a quality that he shares with Berlioz. It is a mistake to compare the music of either of these men with that of Beethoven. One is always being told that Mahler was no Beethoven. Quite so. The difference between listening to Beethoven and listening to Mahler is the difference between watching a great man walk down the street and watching a great actor act the part of a great man walking down the street. The two experiences can be equally impressive, though in different ways. Those who dislike Mahler do not enjoy "play acting." One wishes that they had the wit to see that fact and not continue to explain that Mahler was no Beethoven.

Mahler's faults as composer have been dwelt upon *ad nauseam*. Admittedly, he is long-winded, trite, bombastic; he lacks taste, and sometimes he plagiarizes unblushingly, filching his material from Schubert, Mozart, Bruckner, or any other of a half dozen of his favorites. It is music that is full of human frailties, no doubt. But when all is said, there remains something extraordinarily touching about the man's work, something that makes one willing to put up with the weaknesses. Perhaps this is because his music is so very Mahler-like in every detail. All his nine symphonies are suffused with personality—he has his own way of saying and of doing everything. The irascible scherzos, the heaven-storming calls in the brass, the special quality of his communings with nature, the gentle melancholy of a transitional passage, the gargantuan *Ländler*, the pages of an incredible loneliness—all these, combined with the above-mentioned histrionics, an inner warmth, and the will to evoke the largest forms and the grandest musical thoughts, add up to one of the most fascinating composer-personalities of modern times.

From the standpoint of this survey, however, Mahler would be an important figure even if his music were not so engrossing as I believe it to be. Two facets of his musicianship were years in advance of their time. One is the curiously contrapuntal fabric of the musical texture; the other, more obvious, his strikingly original instrumentation. Viewed properly, these two elements are really connected. It was because his music was so contrapuntally conceived, without the typical 19th-century habit of underpinning the melodies with blocked-out harmonies such as we find continuously in Rimsky-Korsakov or Franck—it was because Mahler worked primarily with a maze of separate strands independent of all such chordal underpinning—that his instrumentation possesses that sharply etched and clarified sonority that may be heard again and again in the music of later composers. Mahler's was the first orchestra to play "without pedal," to borrow a phrase from piano technique. The use of the orchestra as a many-voiced body in this particular way was typical of the age of Bach and Handel. Thus, as far as orchestral practice is concerned, Mahler bridges the gap between the composers of the early 18th century and the Neoclassicists of our own time.

In Mahler's music, the timbre of the orchestra is, of course, entirely his own. His scores are full of orchestral *trouvailles*. The many years he spent as conductor of leading orchestral ensembles taught him how to manage with complete assurance unusual combinations of instruments, sudden unexpected juxtapositions of sonorities, and thinly scored passages of instruments playing far apart in their less likely registers—effects that are to be found again in the orchestral works of Schoenberg, of Honegger, and of more recent composers like Shostakovitch and Benjamin Britten.

Speaking generally, one might say that Mahler was a late Romantic making use of an 18th-century technique. Thus, whatever we may think of him as a composer in his own right, it is impossible to deny his influence, direct or indirect, on many of our present-day composers.

Richard Strauss, by comparison with Mahler, cuts a 19th-century figure. One would like to lean over backward in order to be fair in evaluating the work of a man who held the center of the European musical stage from 1890 to 1900. The critical estimate of Strauss has sunk so low in recent years that it is difficult to keep in mind the fact that the tone poems on which his reputation rests were once astonishingly "modernistic." A whole generation of listeners argued the merits and shortcomings of this music. All audiences were agreed on one point, however—that

Strauss's orchestral powers were superb. Without wishing to belittle the obvious brilliance with which the composer handles the orchestral medium, we can no longer share the enthusiasm it first aroused for the simple reason that our taste in instrumentation has undergone considerable change. To us, the general sound of Strauss's orchestra is overrich. His scores are uneconomical, weighted down with notes, super-Wagnerian in effect. They have little relationship to the more sober and precise orchestration of the present day.

Strauss's career followed a course that ran parallel with that of the decadent Romantic movement itself. He did his best work, after reaching maturity, when he was closest in time to Wagner. *Don Juan, Till Eulenspiegel, Death and Transfiguration* are still human and commensurable. *Quixote* and the *Domestic* and *Alpine* symphonies are certainly more astonishing in many ways, but they invariably leave one with a bloated feeling, as of something indigestible and somewhat monstrous. There is very little fun in these scores. They leave one limp but unconvinced.

Nonetheless, it cannot be denied that there are, at moments, in all his work extraordinary premonitions of the music to come. I am thinking of the "critics" section of *A Hero's Life,* which snarls and rasps with all the modernism of a score composed thirty years later. And of certain harmonies in his operas *Salome* and *Elektra,* which are uncompromising in their harshness, and also in *Till Eulenspiegel,* where a few climactic pages are long in advance of the period in which they were conceived. Later composers have used these hints for their own purposes.

But even if these instances are many times multiplied, as I am sure they can be, the essential fact remains—that these are the offspring of an exhausted parentage, and not all Strauss's genius can bring them to life in a way that makes them speak to us of anything but a past world of feeling. For a time the true nature of these tone poems was obscured by long controversies over the relative merits of program versus absolute music. But nowadays there are few commentators who would not agree that the tone poems represent the final manifestation of a dying world—the

Romantic Wagnerian world of the end of the century.

The case of Alexander Scriabin is, in certain ways, a tragic one. The music of this extremely gifted Russian came into being principally by way of Chopin and Liszt. It is, therefore, indisputably Romantic by derivation. But in his later years the composer's music moved from the Romantic to the mystic plane, because of the influence of theosophical ideas that Scriabin had adopted. It is rather curious that no composer before him should have seriously tried to make the connection between music and the occult sciences. More than any other art, music puts us into touch with the unknowable. That is why it has always been associated with religious ritual of all kinds. I suppose, in a certain sense, Scriabin's theosophical mysticism may be considered directly descendant from the Christian mysticism of Wagner's *Parsifal*. In any case, before he died in 1915, Scriabin was planning a so-called *Mystery*, which was to have out-Wagnered Wagner in its amalgamation of all the arts.

Looking at Scriabin's art in its purely musical aspects, one cannot see how it was benefited by the contact with theosophical thought. The composer was at his best in the germinal ideas with which he worked. These are often magical in their effect—the best examples I know of "pure" inspiration. But for some strange reason, Scriabin never succeeded in finding a suitable form for these remarkable themes of his. He never seemed able to free himself from the conservatory lessons of his Moscow days. The ten piano sonatas that he wrote present the incredible spectacle of musical ideas of genius being straitjacketed in the old classical sonata form. It was tragic that Scriabin should have been unable to find the proper form for his musical ideas, for this serious lack is beginning to make performances of even his best works, such as *Prometheus* or the *Poem of Ecstasy*, more and more infrequent.

Harmonically Scriabin's music has had considerable influence, particularly during the period in which it was first being circulated. There was much talk in musical circles then of new scales and their resultant chords. Scriabin's work took a leading place in the discussion because he had developed a system of chordal structure based on a succession of intervals of the fourth instead of the more usual thirds. His harmonies, as a result, were more daring, more sophisticated and subtle than those of most of his contemporaries. But here, again, Scriabin spoiled what he was doing by adhering too closely to a narrow set of self-imposed formulas. Inevitably the pleasurable sensations that were first associated with his harmonic freedom began to wear off as the underlying system became more and more manifest. Even before his untimely death at the age of forty-three, other composers were experimenting with a harmony that was less constricted and more venturesome. By the middle '20s his influence was confined, for the most part, to a small number of admirers inside and outside the Soviet Union. Today, however, it is increasingly evident that the best of his piano pieces are destined to take their place alongside those of Chopin and Liszt as a permanent part of the pianist's repertoire.

Some of my more informed readers may be surprised to find the name of Gabriel Fauré in this list of late Romantics who have influenced present-day music. It is true, of course, that Fauré's influence was confined almost exclusively to France. Nevertheless, as he was head of the Paris Conservatory for fifteen years and the teacher of Ravel, Florent Schmitt, Roger-Ducasse, Nadia Boulanger, and many other leading figures in French musical life, his artistic principles gained broad circulation.

It was during the last twenty-five years of his life, when Fauré had already passed the half-century mark—from about 1898 to 1923—that he really found himself as composer. This means that Fauré's best work was written at a time when Impressionism held the center of the stage in France. Accordingly, interest in his work was quite overshadowed by the more spectacular achievements of Debussy. If he was able to steer a course all his own, completely free of Impressionist influence, it was because of the strongly personal character of his musical nature.

It is not difficult to see why Fauré's example was inspiring to a generation of composers who were quickly tiring of Impressionism. They easily overlooked the fact that Fauré had his roots in the Romantic movement, because his was the pre-Wagnerian brand of Romanticism, without any of the Bayreuth grandeurs. It was almost a kind of neo-Romanticism—delicate, reserved, and aristocratic. Moreover, no matter what its derivation may have been, it possessed all the earmarks of the French temperament: harmonic sensitivity, impeccable taste, Classic restraint, and a love of clear lines and well-made proportions. These qualities shine through even in the earlier works, those that were fashioned too closely after the model of Schumann and Saint-Saëns. What remained uppermost in the minds of Faure's postwar listeners was his directness and simplicity, supplemented by an innate modesty and charm.

His natural medium was the small form: he composed hundreds of songs and much chamber music but comparatively little for orchestra. What Fauré lacked more than anything else to make him a composer of the very first rank was broadness of scope. He worked within a fairly limited emotional frame and tended to depend too much on formulas and sequences of his own contriving. Like Scriabin, but within more normal limits, he was boldest in his use of harmony, discovering subtle modulations and unsuspected relationships between the most ordinary chords. His powers of harmonic invention lasted until he was well past seventy. In songs such as *Diane, Séléné* from *L'Horizon chimérique,* and the *Danseuse* from *Mirages,* in the last piano nocturnes, and perhaps most of all, in the Piano Trio and the second Piano Quintet, he showed himself to be—like the Verdi of *Otello* and *Falstaff*—an example of a septuagenarian at the zenith of his creative powers. These and others of Fauré's late works must be played more often outside France if we are to obtain a more just appreciation of Fauré's influence on the contemporary musical scene.

A great deal of nonsense has been written about the music of Sibelius. It would have been a comparatively simple matter to evaluate the work of Finland's greatest composer if the picture he presents had not been obscured by the exaggerated commentaries of a handful of English and American critics. The simple truth is that Sibelius is a late Romantic composer, with his own personal way of saying things. The only remaining question is, how important are the things that he has to say? My answer would be that they are sympathetic but not very significant for us. Why? Because Sibelius does not live in a 20th-century world. He is a hangover from the 1890s, and although his ruminations on life and man are fairly interesting and are expressed in a purely personal way, they are conclusions arrived at from old-fashioned premises, premises that no longer hold water in our own time.

One asks oneself who first coupled the name of Sibelius with that of Beethoven. They would have been nearer the mark if they had said Smetana or Dvořák. They did the composer an injustice, since they placed him in a position that he fills poorly, and they took emphasis away from his truer qualities. Sibelius is, by nature, a folk composer. Like a folk composer he writes his music our of a special landscape and out of a provincial imagination. There is the constant tendency in him to fall back into a pastoral mood of folk inspiration, to repeat himself in themes and technical formulas, to put us always into the same emotional atmosphere. None of these tendencies is characteristic of the first-rate composer. Within his own limits, however, Sibelius is attractive enough. But there is a difference between being a sympathetic and attractive composer and being the successor to Beethoven, as some would have us believe he is.

Much has been written of the originality of form in the seven symphonies composed by Sibelius from 1899 to 1925. If one were to follow the English critic Cecil Gray, Sibelius is the only composer who has contributed anything significant to the form of the symphony since Beethoven's day. A close examination of the scores themselves will not bear out this assertion. It is certainly to Sibelius' credit that after having written a First Symphony in conventional style, he saw the need for a freer treatment of the symphonic form. As Eric Blom says: "His characteristic method of working with short motives in a kind of mosaic style rather than with elaborate themes which take their recognized places as first, second and auxiliary subjects, would not readily fall into the orthodox formula." At its best the music seems to flower, often from unpromising beginnings. But it is a far cry from having one's own way of doing things to revolutionizing the entire structure of the symphony.

The Fourth Symphony and the Seventh Symphony have elicited most praise from Sibelius' admirers. These works are undoubtedly among his best, but they do not stand up as perfected masterpieces. The Fourth, which was marveled at for its cryptic originality in 1912, is the unmistakable work of the Finnish composer in mood and thematic materials. But the formal structure in several of the movements still seems cryptic today. Similarly, the Seventh, which belongs with the rather rare species of one-movement symphonies, does not satisfy one structurally, being closer in form, despite its name, to the symphonic poem than it is to the symphony. For me, Sibelius is at his best in such moments as the contemplative pastoral mood that opens the Fifth Symphony or in the peasantlike, scurrying passages that begin the last movement of that work, and least impressive in the gloomy, pseudophilosophical broodings of a typically 19th-century mentality.

The attempt to set Sibelius up as the great modern composer of our day is certain to fail, not so much because he falls short of the claims made for him, but simply because his music does not grapple with the problems of our own world. It belongs rather in the post-Tchaikovskian world of the early 1900s. This fact is emphasized by the type of composer that has been influenced by the example of Sibelius. Such men are to be found mostly in countries where his work is played frequently: England, the United States, and, of course, his native land. They are composers who feel lost in the mazes of the contemporary idiom. Sibelius is a refuge to them, since he proves conclusively that a composer need merely treat the materials of music in his own way in order to transfuse the commonest chord or theme with meaning. In that respect his influence has been a salutary one. But insofar as his followers use him as justification for escaping the problems of their own time and place, their work is certain to awaken nothing but echoes of a past era.

The Foreground—Before 1914

⇶ ⇾ ✦ ⇽ ⇷

Schoenberg's Expressionism

THE COMPOSERS whose works have been discussed so far may loosely be said to form the background of modern music. Now we come to that field of new music that still poses listening problems to the uninitiated. Contemporary music, from this time forward, is dominated by two men—Arnold Schoenberg, of Vienna, and Igor Stravinsky, Russian expatriate in Paris.

If it was difficult for composers everywhere to extricate themselves from the Wagnerian cul-de-sac, it must have been doubly so for men like Schoenberg, who were born and grew up in the midst of German music. Schoenberg inherited the full weight of the German tradition; he was the spiritual son of Bruckner, Strauss, and Mahler. He paid them homage in early works like the first songs, the string sextet *Verklärte Nacht*, and the choral symphony *Gurre-Lieder*.

These were the works of a greatly gifted young musician whose mastery of his medium was evident to all. His compositions expanded the language of his predecessors; they contained daring harmonic progressions and an unusual handling of cyclic forms. But they also embodied his own profound attachment to the language and spirit of German music. In the light of his later career, it is ironic to realize how truly conservative Schoenberg was in his instincts and personality. Even the revolution he engendered was made in the name of tradition. Schoenberg himself once wrote: "I claim the distinction of having written a truly new music which, based on tradition as it is, is itself destined to become tradition." Those were prophetic words. Hanns Eisler used to say: "Schoenberg is the true conservative, he even created a revolution so that he could become a reactionary."

Let us see if we can trace the line of his development after the writing of works like *Gurre-Lieder* and *Verklärte Nacht*. Why was he not content to continue writing more such works? The answer can be found in Schoenberg's realization that the tonal system as he knew it was in the process of disintegration. What happened in this composer's harmonic imagination around 1911 was truly unprecedented. With extraordinary boldness, he proposed nothing less than the complete reorientation of our tonal sense.

The basic premise of Schoenberg's harmonic revolution was his denial of our hitherto unquestioned need for the sense of a central tonality. It is difficult, if not impossible, to explain the principle of tonality in nontechnical language, without benefit of live musical illustration. Still, the most untutored musical ear can distinguish something radically "wrong" with Schoenberg's post-Wagnerian harmonies. This sense of "wrongness" comes principally from the lack of any central key feeling.

During the course of the 19th century, music's harmonic language had become richer through more and more chordal complexity. Just think of the difference in sound between the harmonies of Mozart and those of Wagner. It is not a question of whose harmonies are "better," but of a natural historical process based on the physical fact that our ears became attuned gradually to more and more complicated chordal progressions. Thus, starting from a music based on a strong tonal center, with modest modulations, the 19th-century composer moved on to more recondite modulations, until all sense of tonality became ambiguous. Tonal centers in Wagner's music are in such a state of continual flux that even today theorists find much to argue about in analyzing the harmonic structure of his operas.

Up to this point, we can divide Schoenberg's work into two phases: first, the gradual breakdown of tonality as an organizing principle, and second, the frank adoption of an atonal harmonic language.

It took only one logical step forward to achieve a music without tonal center of any recognizable kind. It was a small step—but a crucial one. Only a daring and self-convinced composer could take it, and Schoenberg accepted the role with all its consequences. To other composers it meant that now each tone of the chromatic scale was to be considered of equal importance. It meant, further, the end of consonance and dissonance in the old sense or, as Schoenberg himself put it, "the emancipation of the dissonance." But most important of all, it meant the end of musical structure as we had known it, since structure had as a fundamental basis the orderly progression of harmonies belonging to a recognizable tonal system.

It is not clear to what extent Schoenberg realized at first the full implication of the course he had taken. Trusting his musical instinct, he wrote a series of works between 1907 and 1913 which are strikingly original and inspired: the Second String Quartet (with voice); the piano pieces, Opus 11 and Opus 19; the *Five Orchestral Pieces*, Opus 16; the *Book of the Hanging Gardens,* a setting of poems by Stefan George, for voice and piano; and especially *Pierrot lunaire.*

Aesthetically these works belong with the hyperexpressive paintings of Kandinsky and Kokoschka, the tense and tortured world of Franz Kafka and *The Cabinet of Dr. Caligari.* The movement these artists represented became known as Expressionism; an exaggerated and almost hysterical Romanticism characterizes their work, with prophetic presentiments of the Age of Anxiety that was to follow. These strong works of Schoenberg's second period have, with one exception—the Second String Quartet—one characteristic in common: they are all made up of a series of brief movements. It is as if the composer, at that time, equated extreme emotionality with brevity, sometimes even extreme brevity. The reason is clear: without benefit of the underpinning of a clarified harmonic structure, an atonal work of any length is in danger of falling apart. (Incidentally, Schoenberg objected to the word "atonal" on semantic grounds, but rightly or wrongly, the word has continued in general use to describe this period of his music.) Ernst Krenek speaks of "the unbridled, expressive, and often terrifying outburst of pent-up energy in the early days of atonality."

The most striking and influential work of this period is without doubt *Pierrot lunaire*. It holds a position in Schoenberg's output analogous to that of the *Rite of Spring* in the work of Stravinsky. Both were written at about the same time, around 1912. *Pierrot lunaire* is a series of twenty-one songs for a "speaking voice" and a chamber ensemble of five performers. James Huneker, who was present at its first performance, tells us of the strange impression this composition made on its first listeners in 1913. One wonders what astonished them most—the curious vocal line, half spoken and half sung, the total lack of any recognizable tonal bearings, the thinly stretched and strained sonorities, the complexities of texture, or the almost neurotic atmosphere engendered by the music itself.

Whatever else may be said about it, *Pierrot lunaire* is without question original music. The harmonic daring of the work has no precise precedent in any other music; it bespeaks an extraordinarily keen aural imagination. Out of the few instruments called for, Schoenberg extracts an incredible variety of instrumental imagery—and with the greatest economy of means. It marks the beginning of a subsequent development: the writing by other composers of works for a varied assortment of instruments in small ensemble groups. Texturally, there is strong emphasis on the independence of contrapuntal lines. The complex web of sound is firmly based on known strict forms such as passacaglia, fugue, and canon. The *Sprechstimme*, a curious elecutionary use of the voice, here occurring for the first time, was employed again by Schoenberg in later works and by many younger composers. Perhaps one should add that, as sometimes happened with Schoenberg, he was none too happy in his choice of texts, in this instance by the Belgian poet Albert Giraud. The poems, concerning a moon-drunk Pierrot, have faded; nevertheless, with these poems as pretext, Schoenberg created a phantasmagoria that has retained its freshness. (A work such as Pierre Boulez' *Le Marteau sans maître* is unthinkable without *Pierrot lunaire*.)

A lesser composer than Schoenberg would have been content to write more such works. But as a good German, with the German passion for order and systematic thinking, Schoenberg was faced with the necessity of bringing logic and control to the disconcerting freedom of atonality. That this was not easy to do we can deduce from Schoenberg's subsequent silence of eight years. During this period he brought to the problem his gift as theoretician and thinker, and evolved, as he called it, "a method of composition with twelve tones," which we shall discuss at some length in a later section.

Stravinsky's Dynamism

AROUND 1910, the only other practically unknown musical figure comparable in importance to Arnold Schoenberg was Igor Stravinsky, then a recent arrival in the French capital. To appreciate fully the originality of Stravinsky's contribution, one must keep in mind a picture of musical life in Paris at that time. Impressionism was the order of the day. Debussy and his self-appointed Impressionist disciples were the unquestioned musical leaders of the period. They had engulfed all new music in a kind of luminous fog. Most foreign composers who visited the French capital were soon lost in the exquisitely shimmering half lights of the Impressionist school. But apparently the diminutive Igor was too thoroughly Russian to adapt himself to French ways. And so, before many years had passed, it was the Frenchmen who were aping the musical practices of this lone Russian.

Heading the list of Stravinsky's original gifts was his rhythmic virtuosity. Nothing like it had ever been heard in Paris. It has already been pointed out in connection with Mussorgsky that rhythm was not the forte of the Romantic school. With few exceptions (notably Schumann and Brahms), 19th-century composers were thinking principally about harmony or melody or form, least of all about rhythm. And so their rhythmic schemes were generally of the square-cut, unimaginative kind, like those used in a march. Once the rhythmic pattern was started it tended to remain the same. Even Debussy did little more than make his rhythms less rigid. It was Stravinsky who first revitalized our rhythmic sense. He gave European music what amounted to a rhythmic hypodermic. It has never been the same since.

Stravinsky's rhythmic innovations were principally of two kinds: either he played on the repetition of certain definite rhythms with all the insistence of a wild-eyed Tartar, producing in the listener a kind of intoxicated rhythmic trance, or instead of confining himself to the more conventional metrical units of 2, 4, or 6, he exploited unusual rhythms of 5, 7, or 11. Even when retaining the normal 2, 4, or 6 units, he alternated these abruptly. "Such a procedure looks something like this: ONE-two, ONE-two-three, ONE-two-three, ONE-two, ONE-two-three-four, ONE-two-three, ONE-two, etc. Now read that in strict tempo as fast as you can. You will see why musicians found Stravinsky so difficult to perform when he was new. Also, why many people found these new rhythms so disconcerting merely to listen to. Without them, however, it is hard to see how Stravinsky could have achieved those jagged and uncouth rhythmic effects that first brought him fame." * Thus, something of the barbaric and unspoiled vigor of primitive rhythms found their way into European music during this period.

This extraordinary rhythmic puissance Stravinsky owes to his Russian heritage—to the folk songs of his country, the music of Mussorgsky and Borodin and of his teacher Rimsky-Korsakov. Later on he was to add still another potent device to his rhythmic scheme, a device borrowed from or suggested by American jazz—the combination of two or more simultaneous and independent rhythms. But of this more later.

In the ballets written about this time—*The Firebird, Petrushka, The Rite of Spring*—the musical world of 1910 became

* Quotation from the chapter on Rhythm in my book *What to Listen for in Music,* New York, 1939.

aware of a new type of harmony. Here for the first time we find that bold use of dissonance that is characteristic of so much later modern music. One can only marvel at the rightness of Stravinsky's instinct in handling these new and unprecedented chordal conglomerations. His deliberate choice of shrilly dissonant tonal mixtures shocked and delighted a new generation of music lovers, at the same time revolutionizing the composer's harmonic stock in trade.

Stravinsky's dissonances have very little relationship, of course, to the atonal writing of Schoenberg, except that both composers immeasurably widened our conception of harmonic possibilities. In the Russian's work the tonal texture is much more closely akin to that of our normal harmonic system. What he did was merely to extend that system. This extension brought with it only one new harmonic device, namely, the combining of two or more independent tonalities at the same time. This came to be known as polytonal harmony.

Unlike Schoenberg's atonal system, which attempts to break down our ideas of tonality, polytonality is in a real sense a re-affirmation of the old principles of harmony, but in a new guise. No one has tried to set up any logical system based on polytonal writing. For the most part, composers have used it in an incidental way, rather than trying to apply the principle consistently in large works.

One other important facet of Stravinsky's new style—one admired even by his early detractors—is the masterly way in which the modern orchestra is handled. The Italian composer Malipiero pointed out that even an old orchestra would sound transformed into a modern one if it were given Stravinskian harmonies and rhythms to play. But there is more than these to the clean brilliance of Stravinsky's instrumentation. His stunning effects are mostly arrived at through a careful choice of unhackneyed instrumental combinations, balanced and juxtaposed in such a way as to keep their separate tonal values clearly distinguishable in the orchestral mass. In these early works Stravinsky chooses sharply defined colors not unlike the strong reds and browns of a modern painter. His new orchestral sonorities have little affinity with either the overlush orchestra of Strauss or the overrefined Debussian orchestra. Once again, as in Mahler, the orchestra plays "without pedal." It produces a hard, dry, crackling sonority unlike anything to be heard in previous music.*

Stravinsky borrowed his melodies liberally, during this first period of his career, from Russian folk song. Short, simple folk phrases are put through a Stravinskian formula that has them turning about themselves in a manner peculiar to the composer. It is these plain tunes that make Stravinsky's music sound so very Russian. They are also responsible for the accusation, heard repeatedly, that Stravinsky seriously lacks any real melodic invention. In line with this reproach, which is not without foundation, it is curious to see how, in later works, Stravinsky managed to supply himself with melodic material, even after he had abandoned the use of native Russian folk melodies.

All these startling innovations in rhythms, harmonies, and orchestral timbres were obvious even to a casual listener. What was less obvious at the time was the historic role Stravinsky's ballets were to play in the reorientation of music away from the German tradition. True enough, anyone could see that there was something brutally unsentimental that separated this music from music of the Romantic era. By comparison, this new music seemed blunt, direct, and nonerotic. People were right in calling the young Stravinsky a sophisticated primitive. Even the relationship of Stravinsky to the Russian world of Mussorgsky and his colleagues was clear enough. But only today are we able to see

* It is interesting to compare Stravinsky's orchestral methods with those of Arnold Schoenberg, who achieved an orchestral style of his own, ideally suited to the hypersensitive quality of his music. This he accomplished by applying the chamber-music technique to the large orchestra. Instead of dividing the seven notes of a given chord among seven instruments of the same group, he carefully distributed them among instruments of different groups, thereby gaining the richest possible texture for each chord. Characteristic of one small corner of his orchestration is the love of a magical, bell-like sonority that is somehow extracted from harp, celesta, glockenspiel, mandolin, and so forth. Alban Berg took full advantage of that hint in his last orchestral works.

the connection between this music of Stravinsky's and the eventual goal of objectivism that was to dominate a large segment of the contemporary musical movement.

It is not necessary to be a profound student of music to realize that a close parallel exists between the realistic approach of Mussorgsky in the creation of his protagonist Boris Godunov and the attitude of Stravinsky in the creation of his puppet Petrushka. There is a clear distinction between their approach and that of Wagner, for instance, in the creation of his Tristan. When we listen to Wagner's opera we seem to be hearing the voice of Wagner himself speaking through the stage character of Tristan, but when we listen to Mussorgsky's Boris we seem to be hearing the voice of an entire people. In a similar way, although on a lesser plane, one never for a moment can imagine Petrushka as a mouthpiece for an expression of Stravinsky's personal emotions. The composer in this case cannot possibly be identified with his puppet hero. He seems to feel for and sympathize with Petrushka, standing on one side of the stage and contemplating, as it were, the pitiful antics of the puppet, much in the way that the audience itself is moved by the little tragedy. In other words there is an objective quality in the composer's attitude that separates it completely from the 19th-century Romantic attitude. This desire for objectivity developed later, as we shall see, into the conscious adoption of a Neoclassic style.

The key work of this period is, by common consent, Stravinsky's ballet of pagan Russia, *The Rite of Spring*, composed for Sergei Diaghilev's Ballet Russe in 1913. This is not the composer's most perfect work, but it is certainly his most strikingly original composition. An almost hieratic atmosphere is evoked—coldly mystic and calculatingly savage by turns. Here again the detached spirit I speak of is clearly discernible. The formal structure is the least successful aspect of the work, which, because of its explosive nature, tends to be disjointed. Stravinsky was consciously avoiding, no doubt, the usual German procedures for developing a piece of music, but he had as yet no clear plan of his own to substitute for them.

The Rite of Spring is the last of Stravinsky's large works that has its roots partly in the Romantic movement. Despite the generally detached spirit, there are certain Romantic traits: the lushness of texture in the opening sequence, the tonal painting in the seduction scene, the sense of the enactment of elemental emotions, and the overpowering climaxes of sound—all these are not unrelated to the sonorous magnificences of Strauss or the early Ravel. The works that were fully emancipated from the Romantic strain were to come later.

Béla Bartók

IN A REVIEW OF this important prewar period, the name of the Hungarian composer Béla Bartók must figure prominently. He belongs with Stravinsky and Schoenberg as one of the leading spirits of the new musical movement. Bartók was both lucky and unlucky in his background. He was lucky in his inheritance of an untouched native source material. He and his compatriot Kodály spent years in searching out, collating, and utilizing native Hungarian melodies. Bartók was the best of the folklorists, using his indigenous material as the basis for a music that is both high in quality and very characteristic of the modern musical school.

But Bartók was far from lucky in gaining recognition for his pioneering efforts in the contemporary idiom. He, too, wrote polytonal harmonies, as early as 1908; he, too, was expressive in the tortured manner of Schoenberg, and felt at least as much at home in rhythmic intricacies as Stravinsky. But for some reason these other men were more successful in enlisting the public's attention and in gaining credit with critics and commentators for the introduction of new musical methods.

Perhaps one reason why Bartók did not figure more prominently during this time is the lack of one or more imposing works to dramatize and summarize his achievements. The list of his compositions includes an opera, a ballet, several orchestral works, six string quartets, and much piano music, but does not include any one work such as *Pierrot lunaire* or *The Rite of Spring* to symbolize his output for the public at large. But there are other reasons, also, reasons inherent in the man himself. Bartók's very individual style turned out to be a kind of stumbling block to his full development. I agree with Paul Rosenfeld when he writes: "His [Bartók's] mind has gone into subtlety and intricacy more than range and scope of experience." This tendency toward self-repetition, both of mood and of technical device, made some of his work less inventive and exciting than it should have been.

Bartók's musical style lends itself well to literary description, not because of any programmatic content but because of its highly graphic nature. His music is of a dry, unsentimental facture, full of incisive rhythms and sharp harmonic dissonances. Quite special to Bartók are his slow movements. These have a certain shell-shocked atmosphere, profoundly pessimistic in tone. The Second String Quartet, written during the darkest years of the First World War, is characteristic of this mood, with its bitter harmonies and cheerless melodies. It is deeply expressive music, making no concession to mere prettiness. In his last years, Bartók became an indefatigable explorer in clangorous sonorities. When these are applied to music in slow tempo, a highly personal, rock-like quality results, relentless and uncompromising from the standpoint of audiences brought up on Romantic music.

All his music is intelligently made, almost diagrammatic in conception. Sometimes this proves a pitfall for the composer— when his interest in the formal plan and its realization on paper seem to outweigh the purely musical interest. This danger is also inherent in Bartók's love of tonal effects. A work such as the Fifth String Quartet, remarkable as it is in technical handling of the musical materials, sometimes gives us ingenious manipulation of notes in lieu of spontaneously conceived music. But when he is at his best, as in the *Music for Strings, Percussion, and Celesta,* Bartók takes his place in the front rank of contemporary musicians.

1967: In retrospect I was right to have been mystified as to why Béla Bartók did not reach a larger public during his lifetime. His public image has entirely changed. For reasons difficult to fathom, his death in 1945 set off a chain reaction that gave him, within a few years, his rightful place in the forefront of contemporary music everywhere. Works that had long been admired by forward-looking musicians, but infrequently played, have become firm repertory items. I am thinking of the six string quartets, the Violin Concerto, and especially the 1943 Concerto for Orchestra. These works have not changed, but public acceptance has mellowed. It is an all too familiar phenomenon: the disappearance of the creator coincides with the resurrection of his work.

Music between the Wars (1918-1939)

Music after the First World War

THE MUSIC that has been discussed so far was rudely interrupted in its natural growth during the four years of the First World War. The war years isolated composers so that they lost contact with one another. Schoenberg, Stravinsky, and Bartók worked alone, and their compositions had only local circulation.

But once the war was over, an extraordinary period of musical activity set in. It was as if four years of musical starvation had engendered an insatiable hunger to find out what all the composers in the different countries had been doing. By 1920 a whole batch of new composers had appeared on the musical scene—some who were just beginning to be known before the war intervened and were now grown to full musical maturity, others who had been students during the lean war years and were now ready to make their bid for fame. A mere list of these men is impressive: Falla in Spain, Bloch in Switzerland, Szymanowski in Poland, Malipiero in Italy, Kodály in Hungary, Berg and Webern in Austria, Hindemith in Germany, and last, but far from least, the Group of Six in France (Milhaud, Honegger, Poulenc, Auric, Tailleferre, Durey).

It was a period during which composers were frankly out to do original things. A healthy spirit of investigation pervaded all musical activity. Among many other kinds of interests, the ironic and grotesque seemed to exert a particular fascination. No combination of instruments was too outlandish to be tried at least once. There were experiments in jazz, in quarter-tone music, in music for mechanical instruments. Composers vied with one another in damning all conservative music. Each new composition was accompanied by copious explanations as to its newness, as if that alone were justification for its existence. Taken all in all, it was an eventful and lively period, even though the results did not always lead anywhere in particular. The wonder is that so much that is good remains.

After the war the center of musical activity definitely shifted from Germany to France. This gradual swing away from Central Europe had been gaining momentum ever since 1900, and by 1920 Paris was the leading spirit in all new musical things. The bitterness engendered by the war accelerated the pace at which French composers were freeing themselves from the dominance of German music. They became more and more conscious of their own purely Gallic tradition in music, a tradition that antedates the Romantic movement by many years. This fact is of especial significance, of course, in tracing the pull-away from the German hegemony in music.

Whatever happened in France was of importance to the rest of the musical creative world. By the time the war was over, Impressionism was no longer the "latest thing." The musical field was taken over by two factions: one led by Debussy's younger contemporaries Maurice Ravel and Albert Roussel, who were, in effect if not in name, the leaders of a post-Impressionist movement; and the other consisting of still younger men—the anti-Impressionists, one might call them—led by that curious and legendary figure Erik Satie.

Ravel and Roussel

NOWHERE can we see the change that had come over the aesthetic ideals of new music better than in comparing the late works of Ravel and Roussel with those of their great predecessor Debussy. Ravel and Roussel were both attacked at first as being mere imitators of the older man. This was true, I suppose, to a limited extent: they borrowed his musical vocabulary, and especially in their youthful works, were attracted by the Impressionist theory. But both Ravel and Roussel were born with distinctive personalities of their own. Their mature music leaves no possibility for confusion; for where Debussy is vague and poetic Ravel and Roussel are precise and *spirituel*. In the end, they both succeeded in adapting Debussy's innovations to their own purposes, and it is only in that sense that they are post-Impressionists.

The essential Classic approach is present in the construction of their music. The musical line is built up carefully, with an unerring instinct for the proportion of the whole. There are no loose ends, no details unaccounted for. The characteristics of reticence, of perceptivity and refinement, of expert craftsmanship—all so typically French—are all there; but combined with them is an open-eyed lucidity about the function and meaning of the music that bespeaks a detachment on the part of the composer that is the antithesis of the Romantic attitude. In certain ways, one might say that the later symphonies of Roussel and the concertos of Ravel owe something to the symphonies and concertos of Saint-Saëns or to the chamber music of Faure. But whereas these two older men were writing French music within a German framework, Ravel and Roussel were composing their works with a strong sense of relationship to the purely French traditions of a Couperin or a Rameau.

Here the similarities in the music of Ravel and Roussel end. If the young men of the '20s bitterly attacked Ravel on occasion, it was because they saw in his music little reflection of the disabused and hard new postwar world. The sensuousness and sheen of all Ravel's music, the desire to allure and charm, the calculated brilliance and virtuosity, all seemed somehow to be part of the comfortable bourgeois world of prewar days. One ought not to forget also the natural tendency on the part of the young to decry anything so powerfully attractive as the music of Ravel. They intuitively fear its influence. For Ravel certainly had admirers aplenty and imitators, also. Even today, it is not easy to determine exactly where Ravel belongs in the musical cosmos or how viable the future may prove his music to be. Perhaps its very perfection makes us unduly suspicious of the actual musical content. Despite the fact that his music may not cut very deep, no contemporary composer possessed a more integrated style nor a greater passion for the sheer sensuousness of musical sounds. For that we should be thankful.

Roussel fared better at the hands of the young, even though they must have known that he was by nature a less gifted composer than Ravel. But despite his somewhat artificial style, they undoubtedly sensed an inner freshness of spirit. Roussel's is music that does not give up its secret easily. The curiously strained harmonies, the slightly (always slightly) awkward melodies, the brisk but unspontaneous rhythms, the generally acidulous quality that surrounds all his mature work do not gain him easily won friends. But Roussel's work, to the initiated, exerts a fascination of its own. There is an objective and healthy, almost happy, athleticism about his later compositions, such as the Third Symphony, the Suite in F, and the Sinfonietta for strings. In these pieces Roussel left far behind him the nebulous Debussian aesthetic and attached himself to the more advanced tendencies of the day.

Satie and "Les Six"

ONLY ONE COMPOSER succeeded in attracting to himself the unreserved approval of a small but choice coterie of younger men—Erik Satie. The role of Satie in French music is not unlike that of Busoni in Central Europe. In each case the influence of the man as a leader of the avant garde was perhaps more important than the significance of the music that he himself wrote.

The Satie influence showed itself at first through the work of the Group of Six—particularly in the music of Georges Auric, Francis Poulenc, and Darius Milhaud. The formation of this group had been fortuitous and the association was continued purely as a matter of expediency. The Six decided that they could more easily get a hearing for their work as a unit than as individuals. Erik Satie was their spiritual godfather, and his ideas on music and art were often made manifest through the writings of the young French critic Jean Cocteau.

It is amusing to realize that in his own very French way, Satie was something of a crusader. He set himself against all music that took itself too seriously. He had his own way of crusading—it consisted of poking quiet fun at all officialdom, musical and otherwise. He had the "firmest conviction," as Virgil Thomson puts it, "that the only healthy thing music can do in our century is to stop trying to be impressive." Since almost all music tries for impressiveness in one way or another, we can appreciate how large a crusading job Satie had undertaken.

He indicated the direction he thought new music should take by writing numerous short pieces of a disarming simplicity and an extraordinary rightness of musical feeling. Then he tried to put one off the track by adding whimsical titles (satirizing Debussy's poetic names for pieces), posing as a revolutionist by occasionally leaving out barlines, and imposing idiotic directions for playing in every other measure. "To the uninitiated they [these pieces] sound trifling. To those that love them they are fresh and beautiful and firmly right." I am quoting Thomson again. In an illuminating article on Satie's work he continues: "And that freshness and rightness have long dominated the musical thought of France. Any attempt to penetrate that musical thought without first penetrating that of Satie is fruitless."

Thomson's claim is that Satie invented the only 20th-century musical aesthetic in the Western world. Everything else, by comparison, is old stuff. By eschewing "the impressive, the heroic, the oratorical, everything that is aimed at moving mass audiences" and valuing instead "quietude, precision, acuteness of auditory observation, gentleness, sincerity and directness of statement" Satie showed us how to cut the Gordian knot that ties all music to the shopworn Romanticism of the preceding century. All this is no doubt implicit in the short and unpretentious works of Satie himself. But it might be argued that being simple and direct in one's work might better be set down as a question of temperament and cannot reasonably be blown up to the proportions of a world aesthetic.

However we may judge the connotations of Satie's example, the Six and many younger composers seized upon it as a program for French music. Through it they were going to free themselves not only of the Romantic taint but of the earmarks of Debussy, Ravel, and all their Impressionist confreres.

The Six symbolized a new 20th-century type of composer. They ended forever (we hope) the 19th-century conception of composers as long-haired geniuses who live and starve in garrets. To the Six the creative musician was no longer the high priest of art but a regular fellow who liked to go to night clubs like everybody else. What they wanted to write was "une musique de tous les jours"—a more everyday kind of music. Not the kind that you listen to with your head in your hands, lost in reverie or some sort of emotional fog. All that was ended. We were to listen now with eyes wide open to music that was "down to earth," as Hollywood would say.

All this, whatever else it may have been, proved to be a very effective means for calling attention to a group of unknown composers. The air became charged with musical polemics. The established critics, particularly those who had championed the cause of the Impressionists, became angry and gave the Six even more publicity than they had hoped for. As for the composers themselves, they turned out to be a variegated set of new talents. Francis Poulenc hewed closest to the Satie line, particularly in his first works; Auric wrote a pungent and witty music—somewhat dry and ascetic in quality; Tailleferre could not quite pull herself away from the attractions of Impressionism; and Durey shortly dropped out of sight altogether. It was clear from the start that the two leading members of the group were to be Arthur Honegger and Darius Milhaud.

Of all the group, Honegger was the least affected by the Satie shibboleths. His Swiss origin, and frequent visits to Zurich, left him not untouched with a Teutonic love of the grandiose. He is at his best in large dramatic works—operas and oratorios, like *King David* and *Antigone*—that give his generous gifts full opportunity to spread themselves. For a time, he held the center of the stage as far as new music was concerned. But despite its not in-considerable qualities, Honegger's music is essentially conventional. He was an important figure in those early postwar years, if only because he made palatable to many listeners a new type of musical language that somehow seemed justified when used to illustrate the pathetic and biblical subject matter of his large choral frescoes. But his music has not worn well. Perhaps it is because he was so well understood then that his music has less attraction for us now.

The Lyricism of Milhaud

MILHAUD, on the other hand, had himself partly to blame for the lack of sympathy that enveloped his music when it was new. He quickly gained the reputation of a man who delighted in antago-nizing people. His music was more dissonant, his critical reviews were more outspoken, and his general revolutionary tenets were more violent than those of any of the other young radicals who grouped themselves around Satie and Cocteau in 1919. To the majority he seemed a noisy and aggressive upstart; to others more kindly disposed he was an amusing fellow, full of life and verve, but essentially a *blagueur*. It has taken more time than one would have thought necessary to demonstrate a fact that should have been clear from the start, namely, that Milhaud was the most im-portant of the new generation of composers in France.

It was not appreciated at first, either, that Milhaud's musical style is by nature essentially lyric. His music always sings. Whether he composes a five-act opera or a two-page song, this singing quality is paramount. The music flows so naturally that it seems to have been improvised rather than composed. What Milhaud writes comes from the "deep places of the mind"—from a kind of secondary consciousness over which he seems to exert no control.

This utter simplicity of approach has resulted in a style uniquely and unmistakably his own. You can distinguish a page of Milhaud from among a hundred others. Unlike Stravinsky or

Schoenberg, who each evolved an individual speech gradually, Milhaud is recognizably himself in his earliest compositions. This did not prevent him from submitting himself to a series of widely differing influences: first Debussy; then, with a two-year stay in Brazil, the popular melodies he heard there; later Stravinsky; then jazz; then Satie. No matter—whatever he touches receives his imprint. Sometimes there is a repetition of certain favorite harmonic and rhythmic formulas. But for the most part his homogeneity of style results from the effortless reflection of a distinct personality.

Three moods are characteristic of much of this composer's music: a violently dramatic and almost brutal mood, a relaxed mood of almost childlike gaiety and brightness, and a tender and nostalgic sensuousness. Perhaps it is this last-named trait, with its naïve and all-pervading charm, that makes Milhaud most understandable. To sense it to the full inevitably means that one has come under the spell of the composer. With a quietly moving diatonic melody and a few thick-sounding harmonies he creates a kind of charmed atmosphere. When darkly colored, it takes on a deeply nostalgic connotation. Since this nostalgia is shared by none of his French confreres, I take it to be a sign of Milhaud's Jewish inheritance. That he is not so racial a composer as Bloch or Mahler seems natural if we remember that his ancestors settled in Provence in the 15th century, so that his Jewishness has long been tempered by the French point of view. Nevertheless his subjectivism, his violence, and his strong sense of logic (as displayed in his strict use of polytonality) are indications that the Jewish spirit is still alive in him.

His music can be quite French when it is gay and alert. In this mood his love for simple folklike tunes and clear-cut rhythms is apparent. It is when the harmonies turn acidulous and the rhythms are oddly accented that his gaiety becomes more brusque and truculent. Very personal, also, is the manner in which the music is put together. The textural buildup is peculiarly his own. (To be more specific on this point would lead us into too many technicalities.) Structurally the music is always under control. One never meets with overdevelopment of an idea in Milhaud. He states the core of the matter and then stops.

This last is surprising in a man who possesses so fertile an imagination. A mere listing of his works in all forms is impressive; they include operas, ballets, oratorios, film scores, theater music, music for orchestra and chamber orchestra, concertos, string quartets, a large number of songs, piano pieces, and choral music. No wonder Milhaud has been accused of writing too much. Naturally some of this is repetitious, and not all is of equal value. The sensible thing to do, as with every other prolific composer, past and present, is to choose the best from among his many productions.

First in importance are perhaps the operas and ballets. There are large, impressive stage works such as *Christophe Colomb* (1928) and *Médée* (1939); shorter lyrical dramas such as *Le pauvre matelot* and *Esther de Carpentras;* and tiny chamber operas lasting no more than eight minutes each: *Thesée, Ariane,* and *L'Enlèvement d'Europe.* The ballets range from the early but striking *L'Homme et son désir* through *Salade, Le Train bleu, Les Songes,* and *The Man from Midian* (1940). Perhaps the most charming of the ballets is *La Création du monde,* composed in 1923. Based on a scenario by Blaise Cendrars, it treats of the creation of the world according to African legends. Much of the musical material is lifted from jazz—there are fugues on a jazz subject, a blues section, and a long melody over a "barbershop" accompaniment. Better than any other European, and before hearing Gershwin's famous *Rhapsody* (first performed in the following year), Milhaud understood how to assimilate the jazz idiom.

1967: The past two decades have shown surprisingly little change in Milhaud's production. Since the end of the Second World War, he has been spending alternate years at his teaching post at Mills College in California and at his apartment in Paris, with an annual summer's stay at the Aspen Music Festival, where he functions as head of the Composition Department. One might reasonably suppose that all this extra-compositional activity would inevitably curtail his productivity, but one would be wrong. He has probably produced a greater quantity of viable music (he is now, in 1967, in his seventy-fifth year) than any other living man. Fifteen years ago he had reached his Opus 320; in the last ten years he has added ten symphonies to his list of works. No one would or could expect all of this torrential out-pouring of notes to be of equal interest. But that is just the point: how are we to sort out and hear performed a sufficient portion of Milhaud's production to warrant passing judgment on the totality of the work of the past quarter century? Here is a task for some perceptive investigator that is long overdue. I venture to say that the investigator would find surprisingly little change in the composer's style or language or "message." His musical invention has, at times, turned repetitious, but the general man-ner is as relaxed and unassuming as ever before. He seems to be approaching closer and closer to Satie's ideal of the sweetly human composer with no desire to astonish or overawe his lis-teners. The cold fact is, nevertheless, that in a time like our own, with emphasis on new media, new methodologies, and new aesthetics, Milhaud's late period may quite naturally seem to lack "excitement." No matter. One can confidently expect that a time will come when a sorting process will reaffirm the unique value and range of Milhaud's finest work.

The Jazz Interlude

THE INTEREST OF Milhaud in jazz was, of course, no isolated phenomenon. In fact, the preoccupation with the American dance band when first it arrived in European capitals after the war was widespread. The peak of interest was reached by about 1925. Nevertheless, ever since that time, jazz phraseology has continued to seep into contemporary music to such an extent that a survey of the field would be incomplete without a close examination of the exact nature of its influence.

There is, of course, plenty of precedent in former times for the borrowing by serious composers from popular dance sources. This may have a particular piquancy in the present instance because of the "ordinariness" of jazz by comparison with what is generally thought of as the reconditeness of modern music. Still, no one would deny that a parallel does exist between a composer of the '20s writing a fox-trot and Mozart or Haydn writing a minuet or Chopin a waltz. Only one step further is taken when Beethoven transmutes the minuet into a scherzo or Ravel idealizes a dance form into *La Valse* or the *Bolero*. The serious composer needs freshening occasionally from the less conscious and more naïve springhead of popular or folk music. Otherwise there is the danger that he may dry up, become academic and unimaginative. The contemporary composer's use of jazz had logic and tradition behind it and was more or less to be expected.

It might be added, by way of parenthesis, that the opposite process, in which jazz borrows from the classics—the so-called "swinging" of the classics that gained temporary currency—is less to be encouraged. Not so much because of the bastard versions of the classics that it makes known, though these are tasteless enough, but because it indicates a weakening of invention on the part of our popular composers. It should be discouraged not because it is bad for the classics (they will survive, I imagine), but because it is definitely bad for jazz. It glorifies the arranger at the expense of the tunesmith, whose talents are becoming less and less essential in turning out the Tin Pan Alley product.

When jazz was new a great deal was written about it as an expression of the times we live in. The identification of jazz with the *Zeitgeist* formed the text of many an article during the '20s. What interested composers, however, was not so much the spirit, whatever it symbolized, as the more technical side of jazz—the rhythm, melody, harmony, timbre through which that spirit was expressed.

From the composer's viewpoint, jazz had only two expressions: the well-known "blues" mood, and the wild, abandoned, almost hysterical and grotesque mood so dear to the youth of all ages. These two moods encompassed the whole gamut of jazz emotion. Any serious composer who attempted to work within those two moods sooner or later became aware of their severe limitations. But the technical procedures of jazz had much wider implications, since these were not necessarily restricted to the two moods but might be applied to any number of different musical styles.

By far the most potent influence on the technical side was that of rhythm. No one has been able to trace with any surety the origin of jazz rhythm. It seems safe to suppose that it began long ago on some Negro's dull tom-tom in deepest Africa. In the slave ships of the early traders it came to America, and then, in a new environment, took on different but distinctly related forms in Cuba, in Brazil, and in the United States. In our country we trace jazz rhythm to the minstrel songs of the 1840s and, later, to the spirituals, work songs, and religious "shouts" of the rural Southern Negro. All these related American musical types were crystallized around 1900 into a commercial song-and-dance idiom that went under the name of ragtime.

In 1927 I published an article in the magazine *Modern Music* in which I tried to show the metamorphosis of rhythm in popular music from ragtime to jazz. This analysis has been quoted so often by subsequent writers that I trust I need no further excuse for reprinting it here, at least in part:

"The rhythmic foundation of ragtime is an unchanging 1-2-3-4 bass in quick tempo (stressing the most obvious beats, the first and third). Over the ragtime bass is carried invariably one of two rhythms, sometimes both; either the dotted eighth followed by a sixteenth: ♩. ♪♩. ♪ or this most ordinary syncopation:♫♩♫♩ . The former of these produced the characteristic ragtime jerk which is perhaps best remembered from *Everybody's Doin' It*."

Winthrop Sargeant, in his book *Jazz: Hot and Hybrid*, demonstrates that I neglected to point out one further syncopated rhythm that was a late addition to ragtime and became eventually of crucial importance in its transmutation into jazz. In addition to the syncopation already quoted: ♫♩ (which Sargeant calls the cake-walk syncopation, familiar as long ago

as 1834), we have this less common syncopation: ♪♫♪♫ or
♫♪♫♪ . He concludes, therefore, that from the purely rhythmic
angle, jazz is no more interesting than ragtime. This may be true
from a strictly analytical viewpoint, but the limited use to which
this more complex syncopation was put, plus the relentless insistence of that *1-2-3-4* in the bass, gives to all the early two-steps a
honky-tonk quality that makes early jazz, by comparison, seem
several paces ahead of ragtime in rhythmic sophistication.

All this is parenthetical to my own analysis, which continues
thus:

"Modern jazz began with the fox-trot. For this new dance the
four-quarter bass was used as in ragtime but at a considerably
slower pace and miraculously improved by accenting the least
obvious beats, the second and fourth—*1-2-3-4*. With this was
combined another rhythmic element, sometimes in the melody
but by no means always there, which is generally supposed to be
a kind of 1-2-3-4 and is always written: ♫♫♫♫♫♫ . . . Don
Knowlton was the first to show [*] that this jazz rhythm is in reality
much subtler than in its printed form and is properly expressed
thus: ♫♫♪:♩ ♪:♫ . Therefore, it contains no syncopation; it is
instead a rhythm of four quarters split into eight eighths
and is arranged thus: 1-2-3:1-2-3-4-5, or even more precisely:
1-2-3:1-2-3:1-2. Put this over the four-quarter bass:

and you have the play of two independent rhythms within the
space of one measure. It is the beginning, it is a molecule of
jazz. . . .

"The next step infinitely complicated these, in fact it produced
polyrhythms. In employing two rhythms within one measure jazz
after all merely did something that had been done before, if we

[*] "The Anatomy of Jazz," in *Harper's Magazine*, April 1926.

remember, for instance, the use by older composers of 3/4 against 6/8. But the next era in the jazz age—typified by Zez Confrey's song *Stumbling*—saw independent rhythms spread over more than one measure, over a series of measures:

That is, while the conventional 4/4 bass was retained the melody was put into 3/4 time. . . . Within small limits jazz had achieved a new synthesis in music. . . .*

"Polyrhythms are, as is known, not in themselves an innovation. They have been highly developed among primitive races and have made intermittent, momentary appearances in the works of recent European composers. They have also occurred abundantly in the English madrigals. The madrigal polyrhythms were the result of the madrigal prosody and therefore an intricate deft interknitting in which no single downbeat was too definitely stressed. In a sense, therefore, the madrigal was arhythmic rather than polyrhythmic. In fact, the madrigalists were charged by later English generations with lacking a proper sense of rhythm.

"But the polyrhythms of jazz are different in quality and effect not only from those of the madrigals but from all others as well. The peculiar excitement they produce by clashing two definitely and regularly marked rhythms is unprecedented in occidental music. Its polyrhythm is the real contribution of jazz."

---

* It is this three-over-four that Sargeant claims is already present in ragtime. ". . . it is difficult," he says (p. 117), "to lay hands on a rhythmic formula in jazz that was not represented earlier in ragtime. One often hears the theory advanced that polyrhythm is a characteristic of the former and absent from the latter. Both Don Knowlton and Copland subscribed to it. But the facts do not support it." Whatever the facts prove, it is incontrovertible that serious composers became aware of the polyrhythmic nature of Afro-American music only in its jazz phase, so that it is safe to assume a fundamental difference in the effects produced, even though single units of the device look the same on paper.

The serious European composer was influenced to a limited extent by our popular music even before it had any polyrhythmic implications. When jazz was still ragtime Debussy wrote his *Golliwog's Cake Walk* (1908) and later *Minstrels* (1910). During the war years Stravinsky essayed several pieces in the ragtime manner: *Piano Rag-Music*, *Ragtime* for eleven instruments, and the dance marked "ragtime" in the *Story of a Soldier*. All these pieces make a rather grotesque impression, as if Stravinsky were merely interested in making Cubistic caricatures out of the crudities of jazz. These little compositions have few admirers, but they are interesting as examples of the way in which Stravinsky's musical mind works. By extracting and isolating certain typical ragtime features, such as the "cakewalk" syncopated figure and the dotted eighth followed by a sixteenth rhythm, and juxtaposing these and other stock items in unexpected ways, he produces a kind of extract of ragtime that is more characteristic of Stravinsky than it is of Afro-American music. It is interesting to note, however, that in the opening March of the *Story of a Soldier,* and also in the section that follows, *The Soldier's Violin,* there are strongly marked polyrhythmic passages that are not to be found in earlier works of Stravinsky (not even in *The Rite of Spring,* despite its rhythmic complexities) or in those of any other European composer of the same time. It would seem likely that these could have come only by way of jazz influence.

The only other aspect of popular music that has had an influence on the serious composer comparable to that of its rhythm is the special fascination exerted by the timbre of the jazz band. As far as harmony and melody are concerned, it was jazz that did the borrowing. In these two spheres the early jazz composer worked within a strictly limited area. Occasionally the serious composer makes use of typical jazz cadences and "barbershop" harmonies for their humorous effect, and similarly certain characteristic turns of melodic phrase, exploited over and over again in popular music, are introduced into the vocal line, but these are almost always in pieces written frankly "in the manner of" a blues or fox-trot and are seldom found—as jazz-influenced rhythm and tone color might be—in pieces without any jazz connotation.

The jazz band derived its special color partly from the absence of strings (violins, violas, and cellos). Since these have formed the basic tonal body in the symphony orchestra ever since Haydn's day, their mere omission was enough to give the jazz band a sonority of its own. Added to this was the functional way in which jazz instruments were divided into rhythm instruments (piano, banjo, bass, and drums) and melody instruments (clarinets, saxophones, trumpets, and trombones). On the firm basic pulse of the rhythm section the melody instruments were able to weave an independent melodic and rhythmic counterpoint, which had to be carefully listened to if all the subtleties of tone color and rhythmic variety were to be heard. This description applies, of course, only to the performance of the best jazz bands.

The original and effective sonorities produced by what was in reality a small chamber-music combination without strings gave composers an incentive to experiment with timbres outside the well-known groupings of string quartet, woodwind quintet, flute and strings, and so forth. Thus, in 1923 we find Stravinsky writing an Octet scored for flute, clarinet, and two each of bassoon, trumpet, and trombone. His ballet *Les Noces* was rescored in three different versions, the final one being for four pianos and thirteen percussion instruments. One could easily add other similar examples from the literature of new music. Composers everywhere were attracted by the supervirtuosity of the individual jazz performer, by the extraordinary rhythmic attack of the best brass sections, by unusual timbres produced out of thoroughly familiar instruments, and by the general spirit of freedom and unconventionality surrounding a first-rate band.

The preoccupation with the popular idiom in the principal centers of jazz influence—France, Germany, and England—had expended itself by the end of the '20s. The revival of interest in jazz of the "hot" variety, which came into vogue around 1935 under the new name of swing, has thus far, at any rate, had little effect on serious music. This may be due to the fact that swing is really nothing new, or it may also be due in part to the fact that the most interesting feature of swing is its improvisational character, which is the one element of popular music that cannot be notated properly. It is interesting to note, however, that the deliberate use of more and more dissonant chords in recent swing will result in making the public at large more readily accept the unconventional harmonies of the modern composer. A few more years of such harmonic liberties and Stravinsky's boldest flights in that field will sound quite tame to the man in the street.

In France, besides Milhaud, whose ballet *La Création du monde* has already been mentioned, many composers wrote pieces in the jazz style. Outstanding among these are Ravel in the slow blues of his Violin Sonata, and Honegger in his Concertino for Piano and Small Orchestra. Especially amusing is the final part of the Concertino, with its whiplike cracklings in the brittle piano part over a long and sentimental jazz tune.

In Central Europe the Schoenberg group remained aloof, but the new opera composers like Ernst Krenek and Kurt Weill went in heavily for the music from America. The phenomenal success of Krenek's *Jonny spielt auf*, with its Negro jazz-band-leader hero, encouraged other Europeans to try their hand at this new style of music. The best composition of them all was Kurt Weill's *Three-Penny Opera*, not so much because it added anything to jazz—it was, in fact, much inferior as such to the homegrown variety—but because it used the jazz idiom to mirror the depressed and tired Germany of the '20s in an unforgettably poignant way. It should be mentioned, also, that Paul Hindemith, in his early works, was not beyond dabbling in the jazz manner, and the polyrhythmic element may be traced in much of his later work (particularly in his *Klavierübung*, Opus 37).

To complete the picture, one should add that in the United States serious composers like John Alden Carpenter, Edward B. Hill, and Louis Gruenberg, during the '20s, and Walter Piston, Robert McBride, and Morton Gould, during the '30s, all used jazz with greater or lesser degrees of politeness. (In this list belong several of my own works—especially *Music for the Theatre*, 1925, and the Concerto for Piano and Orchestra, 1926.) While these composers borrowed some of its procedures from Tin Pan Alley, George Gershwin, who began there, brought jazz with him to the concert hall. His works made up in originality and individuality what they lacked in technical finish.

It is safe to say that no living composer has been entirely unaffected by the revitalized rhythmic sense we have all gained through contact with the peoples of the Dark Continent. (Even so Mexican a composer as Carlos Chávez wrote a *Fox* and a *Blues.*) Whether rhythmic counterpoint is to have as profound an effect on Occidental music of the future as melodic counterpoint has had must remain an open question.

1967: In recent times the tables have turned insofar as jazz influence is concerned: jazz has been more influenced by serious music than the other way around. Almost any musical style can be "jazzified"—witness the adaptation of 18th-century Baroque music, Indian ragas, and so on. Performers such as Ornette Coleman and Jimmy Giuffre have abandoned conventional jazz forms and harmonies for the complete freedom of certain kinds of contemporary music. The significance that jazz has assumed, in all its many manifestations, is emphasized by the English critic-composer Wilfrid Mellers in his recent book on American music. He devotes almost half the volume to a discussion of jazz as an independent and essential part of America's musical history.

Serious music, on the other hand, at least in its strictly serial and electronic aspects, has shown little or no interest in making use of jazz-derived elements. Only chance music, with its improvisational and indeterminate factors, has tended to establish a bond, at least of "philosophy," between popular and serious music.

The value of frankly incorporating the present-day progressive type of jazz idiom within the framework of a concert piece has been staunchly defended by Gunther Schuller, an important member of today's middle generation of American composers. Schuller has invented the term "third-stream music" to characterize the marriage of these two musical genres. Moreover,

Schuller goes further and claims that the jazz-inspired works of serious composers in the '20s quite missed the point: in his opinion, jazz is synonymous with improvisation. Or, to put it another way, without improvisation there is no jazz. But it seems only fair to point out that during the '20s it would have been out of the question to expect a symphony player to be able to ·improvise in the jazz manner. Even today, when Schuller wishes to integrate jazz into a symphonic context he must bring into the concert hall or opera house a "jazz combo" to improvise while the orchestra itself plays from the written notes provided by the composer. The California composer Larry Austin has successfully combined serious and jazz idioms in his Improvisations for Orchestra and Jazz Soloists. *By 1962, the date of the first performance, it had become practical for Austin to request his symphonic interpreter to "invent rhythmic designs on given pitches within specified spans of time." Composers like Austin and David Reck make one suspect that the last word has not yet been said on the influence of jazz on serious composition, at least in America.*

The Neoclassic Movement

THE JAZZ INTERLUDE had no permanent effect on contemporary music's trend away from Romanticism. The interest in jazz was temporary, similar to the interest during the same period in the primitive arts and crafts of aboriginal peoples, reflected in contemporary sculpture and painting. In musical terms, it expressed itself primarily in the introduction of complex rhythms, adding to Stravinsky's juxtaposition of different time signatures the new, simultaneous sounding of independent rhythmic units. But few listeners in the early '20s, even among those who considered themselves to be "in the know," were prepared for the final phase of the development we have been following—the conscious adoption of the musical ideals of the early 18th century.

Here again Igor Stravinsky led the way. The French musical world first became aware of this new tendency—referred to in the beginning as "back-to-Bach" movement—with the first performance of the Stravinsky Octet on October 18, 1923. I was in the audience on the night of its premiere at a Koussevitzky concert in Paris and can attest to the general feeling of mystification that followed the initial hearing. Here was Stravinsky, who had created a neoprimitive style all his own, based on native Russian sources—a style that everyone agreed was the most original in modern music—now suddenly, without any seeming explanation, making an about-face and presenting a piece to the public that bore no conceivable resemblance to the individual style with which he had hitherto been identified. Everyone was asking why Stravinsky should have exchanged his Russian heritage for what looked very much like a mess of 18th-century mannerisms. The whole thing seemed like a bad joke that left an unpleasant after-effect and gained Stravinsky the unanimous disapproval of the press. No one could possibly have foreseen, first, that Stravinsky was to persist in this new manner of his, or second, that the Octet was destined to influence composers all over the world in bringing the latent objectivity of modern music to full consciousness by frankly adopting the ideals, forms, and textures of the pre-Romantic era.

From the vantage point of today we can see that this move on the part of Stravinsky was not nearly so arbitrary as it seemed to the audience of 1923. In tracing its origins, one can already detect a certain internationalist aspect in the *Story of a Soldier,* written in Switzerland five years before the Octet. Its march, tango, valse, chorale, and ragtime have a distinctly cosmopolitan flavor in comparison with Stravinsky's early ballets. We must remember, also, that the Bolshevik revolution of the previous year had aroused absolutely no sympathy in the expatriate composer. Perhaps this event contributed to his marked lack of enthusiasm for peasant folk material as a basis for his music from that time forward.

At any rate, his next composition had no Russian tunes. When, in 1919, the impresario of the Ballet Russe, Sergei Diaghilev, suggested that Stravinsky compose a ballet based on fragments of the 18th-century composer Pergolesi, he found him a willing collaborator. For the first time Stravinsky worked with Bach-like materials. All subsequent evidence points to the fact that the ballet that resulted, *Pulcinella,* was a determining factor in the development of his later style—a much more important factor than any of the first spectators of *Pulcinella* could possibly have foreseen.

The years between *Pulcinella* (1919) and the Octet (1923) were marked by a certain indecision. The *Symphonies of Wind Instruments* (1920) is clearly a transitional work—some of its themes point in the direction of the prewar years, and the exceptionally beautiful coda presages the Neoclassic music to come. As for the one-act stage work *Mavra,* composed a year before the Octet, Stravinsky tells us in his *Autobiography* that he deliberately cultivated "the Europeanized tradition of Russian culture." By this he means, of course, the tradition of Pushkin and Tchaikovsky as opposed to the more militantly nationalist school of the Russian Five.

With the composing of the Octet, Stravinsky established the fundamental outlines of all his subsequent Neoclassic work. He posited a new universalistic ideal for music, based on Classic forms and contrapuntal textures, borrowing his melodic material eclectically from all periods, yet fusing the whole by the indubitable power of his own personality. From this time forward there is a complete unity of aesthetic purpose in all his work. Starting with the colorful realism of *Petrushka* and proceeding through the more impersonal primitivism of *The Rite of Spring* and *Les Noces,* Stravinsky became more and more enamored of the objective element in his creative work until, with the writing of the Octet, he completely abandoned realism and primitivism of all kinds and openly espoused the cause of objectivism in music.

That seems to me to be the fundamental fact. Far from representing a "multitude of aesthetic points of view"—a criticism that has been leveled at Stravinsky over and over again—his work shows a clearly unified purpose. Whatever we may think of the music he wrote during the years 1923–1951, there is no denying its logic. It is the objective attitude that is important and forward-looking, rather than Stravinsky's application of that attitude. For one cannot avoid a certain feeling of dissatisfaction with some facets of Stravinsky's work of this period. Despite the seriousness of tone, the elegance of style, and the brilliance of execution that characterize everything Stravinsky does, it is difficult to understand why he should have felt the need to stay so close to Classic models. There is a reactionary tendency discernible here—in the sudden retreat to more normal musical procedure, in the dependence upon 18th-century melodic contours and forms, and in the general paring down of all the revolutionary elements of his earlier work. These later works constitute what is almost a new phenomenon in music—an "art grafted on art." Only a composer with the personality of a Stravinsky could cope with so many self-imposed limitations. Admirable or not, they make secure Stravinsky's place in the history of the music of our time.

Among the finest works in his Neoclassic manner must be listed the choral *Symphony of Psalms* (1930) and the opera-oratorio *Oedipus Rex* (1927). Both of these bear a definite relation to the pagan feeling of *The Rite of Spring*. In 1928 the ballet *Apollo, Leader of the Muses* added a new suavity and sensuousness to the composer's palette. The crowning work of this period was Stravinsky's opera *The Rake's Progress* (1951), written in collaboration with the poets W. H. Auden and Chester Kallman. It epitomizes the composer's thirty-year fascination with 18th-century ideals.

Now, finally, we have reached the logical end of the movement that began with a small group of obscure Russians in the 1870s—the desire to free music from the stranglehold of German Romanticism. It is as if we have gone all the way around a circle that began with Mussorgsky and ended with Stravinsky—a circle that took some fifty years of the most varied and circuitous efforts to complete itself.

(*Stravinsky's subsequent change of manner will be discussed in a later chapter.*)

The Neoclassic Influence

ONE OF THE least predictable aspects of the Neoclassic movement was the extent of its influence. Very few composers remained entirely untouched by contact with its pre-Romantic ideals. Even composers with firmly established styles of their own found a revitalizing principle in the Neoclassic manner. I am thinking especially of men like Manuel de Falla and his Concerto for harpsichord, flute, oboe, clarinet, violin, and violoncello (1926); Alfredo Casella and his *Scarlattiana* (1926); Albert Roussel and his orchestral Suite in F (1926); Francis Poulenc and his *Aubade* (1931); Ernest Bloch and his Concerto Grosso (1925); Heitor Villa-Lobos and his *Bachianas brasileiras* (1928). Composers who were not directly influenced also found in Neoclassicism an incentive for dropping the mechanistic primitivism of their earlier works. Serge Prokofiev, for example, whose *Scythian Suite* and early ballet *The Age of Steel* had been full of realistic dynamism, struck a brand-new lyrical note in his later stage work *The Prodigal Son* (1928). As for the younger men, they unhesitatingly adopted the classicizing manner. An American composer, Roger Sessions, summed up their new ideals in an article written in 1927, as follows:

"Younger men are dreaming of an entirely different kind of music—a music which derives its power from forms beautiful and significant by virtue of inherent musical weight rather than intensity of utterance; a music whose impersonality and self-sufficiency preclude the exotic; which takes its impulse from the realities of a passionate logic; which, in the authentic freshness of its moods, is the reverse of ironic and, in its very aloofness from the concrete preoccupations of life, strives rather to contribute form, design, a vision of order and harmony."

Of all those who profited by the Neoclassic influence, no one knew better how to develop and reshape it for his own ends than the German composer Paul Hindemith. The appearance of Hindemith on the scene in the early 1920s gave fresh hope to all those who had despaired of finding a man capable of instilling new blood into the exhausted German musical tradition. Beginning his career normally enough under the usual influences of Brahms and Strauss, Hindemith quickly assimilated the latest musical fashions as represented by early Stravinsky and jazz. But his own more characteristic style took shape only when it made contact with the Neoclassic movement.

At this point it is necessary to pause for a moment in order to make clear that the 18th-century ideal had had its own champion in Central Europe even before the war years and certainly before Stravinsky had thought of leading anyone "back to Bach." I am not referring to Max Reger, whose heavy-handed, post-Brahmsian turgidities were mistaken at first for a new form of Classicism. The real leader of the anti-Romantics was the German-Italian composer-pianist Ferruccio Busoni, without doubt one of the most original musical minds of the 20th century. It was the Italian side of his background that made Busoni impatient with Teutonic solutions for all music. Ernst Krenek, who was one of Busoni's best pupils, goes so far as to say that ". . . the concept of neoclassicism originated with Ferruccio Busoni. . . . Busoni's great anathema was nineteenth century romanticism. To him the movement seemed foggy, distorted, pretentious, bombastic and formless. Against these characteristics he marshalled the crystal clearness, the cool fire, the lucidity, and the wise economy of the classical composers, especially of Mozart."

Busoni produced no final statement of principles in his various writings on music. He preferred to throw out aphoristic suggestions rather than lay down any specific program for the music of the future. Nevertheless, it was clear, as his biographer Edward J. Dent puts it, that ". . . what he sought to achieve was a neoclassicism in which form and expression may find their perfect balance." We can best judge the results of Busoni's theories from his short works, like the *Comedy Overture* or the *Rondo Arlec-chinesco,* or from the more ambitious operas *Turandot* and *Doktor Faust.* Opinions differ as to the musical value of these works, but it is impossible to deny their importance as generators of new ideas. The relationship between the *Rondo Arlecchinesco* and some of Hindemith's earlier concert music, for example, is unmistakable. The bounding melodic line, the contrapuntal texture, the absence of any sentimental hubbub—the general buildup of the music on Classic principles—all indicate that the Latin ideals of Busoni had taken hold in the most talented representative of young German music.

The well-known German music critic Alfred Einstein is the authority for the statement that the introduction of new ideas in music was bitterly fought in Germany. "Nowhere else," he says, "was this movement initiated under greater difficulties." Still, Hindemith's talent was such that it impressed all listeners, even those who opposed him bitterly. It is hard to see how they could have avoided being impressed by the forthright quality of the man. From the very start the extraordinary vigor and exuberance of the music, and Hindemith's facility and technical equipment, were generally acknowledged. Whether the mood was healthy and robust or sardonic, boisterous, and full of fun, it was always carried off without the slightest trace of affectation. One would have sworn that these qualities were just what was needed to pull German music out of the doldrums.

Nevertheless, many of these first works suffer from being too eclectic. It wasn't until the Neoclassic trend caught up with him that Hindemith knew best how to exploit his natural gifts. He seemed to have an inborn affinity with the craftsmanlike attitude of the 18th-century composer, with his honest desire to do a job simply and well. He seemed to enjoy attacking many of the old problems, finding his own solutions for them. He wrote a kind of linear counterpoint that infused new life into ancient contrapuntal procedures. He composed long and intricate and pseudo-Bachian melodies, accompanying them with unmistakably 20th-century harmonies. His natural bent for rhythmic energy attached itself to the insistent sixteenth-note motion of a Handelian concerto grosso. He renounced all tonal ambiguity, beginning and ending pieces squarely on the tonic. His forms were sharply defined, each section of each piece having its own clear meaning, as in the works of the 18th-century masters.

Among all the compositions of this period in Hindemith's development, my preference goes to *Das Marienleben,* a cycle of sixteen songs for soprano with piano accompaniment, on poems by Rainer Maria Rilke. Here, for the first time, one is conscious of the peculiar beauty of the composer's quiet episodes—a searching, wistful, hopeless quality such as can be found nowhere else in contemporary music. The Concerto for Orchestra and the *Kammermusik No.* 2 for piano solo and twelve instruments should also be mentioned as among Hindemith's best works of this period.

By the time the Third Reich was in the saddle in Germany, Hindemith had lived a very full musical life. He had served as orchestral musician, quartet player, and conductor; he had composed in every known musical form from grand opera and oratorio down to teaching pieces for infants; he could perform passably well on any one of fourteen different musical instruments; and in 1928 he topped off all this by becoming professor of composition at the Hochschule in Berlin.

As it turned out, it was his teaching that most affected his future work. Like all Germans, Hindemith loved orderliness. Sooner or later he was certain to be disturbed by the lack of any logical systematic procedure on the part of the modern composer. How could he correct the compositions of his students with a clear conscience when no one had formulated the laws governing the writing of modern music? Moreover, the time seemed ripe for such an undertaking. The experimental period of contemporary music was definitely on the wane by 1928, and it became possible at least to make a start in the direction of formulating a clear statement of principles underlying all new music.

With characteristic energy Hindemith produced a book, *The Craft of Musical Composition* (*Unterweisung im Tonsatz*), in which he set forth his ideas regarding modern harmony, melody writing, and related subjects. The importance of all this to an understanding of Hindemith's work is that, having put down to his own satisfaction the basic principles governing the composing of music in the new style, he proceeded to correct not only the compositions of his pupils but also his own early compositions (even including *Das Marienleben*) and to make all his subsequent compositions conform to the principles he himself had deduced.

This was a bold step on Hindemith's part: there are very few examples in musical history of the existence of the creator and theorist in one individual. The danger is obvious—given the formula, the creator is likely to underestimate the unconscious part of creation—what André Gide calls "la part de Dieu." Like all very prolific composers, Hindemith had always run the risk of writing music not because he had to but because he was able to. Now it would seem that, whether the works were to have necessity or not, they would at least have logic.

Fortunately, theory or no theory, Hindemith continued to write viable works—at any rate, when he was at his best. Sometimes the formula gets the better of the music, and we are given a series of sonatas for various mediums that present a depressingly homogeneous physiognomy. But in works like the opera *Mathis der Maler,* the four-hand piano sonata, and the *Saint Francis* ballet, we know we are listening to a creative mind that transcends mere methodic formulas.

One might look in vain through all Hindemith's music for any signs of the cruel years through which Germany and all the world passed. On the surface he appears to have continued writing placidly in his accustomed style, indifferent to censure or acclaim. But if one listens more attentively, there seems to be an increasing dependence on what we might call a medievalizing mood— the mood of resignation, of the elegiac tableau—and a corresponding absence of that robust and aggressive manner that was once so typical of Hindemith's work. No doubt it is Hindemith's capacity for ignoring the confusions and cruelties of his day that accounts for his having been able to produce work after work with incredible regularity. And though these compositions often give the impression that he was no longer inventing out of new experience but merely writing from an experience and a formula that had already served him over and over again, we know that at his best he was able to turn out works worthy of one of the finest musical minds of our generation.

1967: It is evident, it seems to me, that in my summary of Hindemith's achievement, written when the composer was forty-six years old, I was not unaware of what one might call the "workhorse" aspect of his nature. The present generation judges him harshly—is, in fact, downright unfriendly. Hindemith is no longer cited among the top men of our time; it is undeniable that a severe downgrading is in process. However, whatever the eventual fate of his more ambitious works, it seems likely that he will continue to live on in the concert hall and the classroom as the composer of many useful and practical compositions written for almost every medium. As years went by, his strongly peda-gogic nature gradually preempted the place once held by his more adventurous creative urge. The works he wrote as inspired composer—such as Das Marienleben *and* Mathis der Maler—*are secure, but they would appear to be fewer than we had once supposed.*

The Depression Years

THE MUSIC OF THE DECADE 1930–40 emphasized the apparent decline of the experimental phase of contemporary music. For almost forty years, music had passed through a series of revolutionary crises, as a result of which all the stultifying "rules" of harmony, rhythmic phrase, and melodic construction had been broken down. By 1930, composers everywhere began to sense the necessity for consolidating the gains made for their art through so many years of experimentation. Like Hindemith, they wanted to "cash in" on the discoveries of the pioneers, to take stock of all the new musical resources that were now at their disposal. Moreover, from the aesthetic standpoint, there was no longer anything to fear from Romanticism; it had been firmly established that new music, in whatever style, was to be objective in attitude, clearly conceived, and contained in emotional expression.

All this was the natural swing of the musical pendulum. In the past, every period of experimentation in music had been followed by a summing-up period. This need for a new "order" in contemporary music was intensified by one very important external factor, namely, the reaction—or more exactly, the lack of reaction—on the part of the audience.

Since Wagner's day it had become axiomatic that the lay listener was by nature slow to comprehend innovations in music. During the very critical years of change that followed the death of Wagner, composers had come to take it for granted that their works could be of interest only to the most forward-looking among their audiences. How could the ordinary music lover, comparatively unaware of the separate steps that brought on the gradual changes in musical methods and ideals, be expected to understand music that sounded as if it came from some other planet? Composers, by the end of the '20s, began to have an uneasy feeling that a larger and larger gap was separating them from their listeners. They would have been dull indeed not to have realized that this lack of contact with any real audience was placing them in a critical situation. Moreover, the additional fact that new music was beginning to "normalize" itself made it seem more than ever desirable and even necessary that an effort be made to regain the active interest in contemporary music of the entire music-listening public.

The only new tendency discernible in the music of the decade 1930–40 can be traced to this feeling of dissatisfaction on the part of composers at the lack of any healthy relationship with their potential public. As a result, two steps were taken: first, many composers tried to simplify their musical language as much as possible, and second, they attempted not only to make contact with audiences in the concert hall, but to seek out music listeners and performers wherever they were to be found—in the public schools and colleges, the teaching studios, and the movie houses, over the air waves, through recordings—anywhere, in fact, where music was heard or made.

Historically, we can find the first signs of this new tendency in Central Europe during the middle '20s. It was quite natural that in a country where music was more highly cultivated than anywhere else, composers should be made painfully aware of their lack of contact with the musically educated public. A typically German solution was tried. Composers, with Paul Hindemith at their head, began to write a music especially addressed to the needs of the musical amateur. This kind of music, later called *Gebrauchsmusik*—literally, music for use—was designed to familiarize nonprofessional performers with musical devices different from those in the classics they knew so well. This first step was encouraged by the German music publishers, who saw in it the possibility of opening new sales in a hitherto untouched market.*
But the value of this first step was purely tactical, for the actual musical content of most *Gebrauchsmusik* was weak. Composers continued to reserve their best thoughts for their "serious" music. Nevertheless, the possibility of establishing contact with the ordinary music lover was first tested here.

At the same time, another move toward reaching the public was made in Germany. This time it was the opera public that was sought after. Kurt Weill and Ernst Krenek, already mentioned in connection with the jazz influence, deliberately went in for "popular appeal" in their stage works. Both these men were highly trained composers, capable of writing in the most abstruse style. But the postwar opera goer in Germany was not the comparatively erudite listener of the preceding epoch. He was completely unprepared to appreciate the atonal complexities of Berg and Schoenberg. By introducing songs in a pseudojazz manner in place of the old-fashioned aria, Weill and Krenek gave their public something they could comprehend. Here again it was

* In a letter to Nicolas Slonimsky from B. Schott's Sons, Hindemith's publishers (quoted by Mr. Slonimsky in his book *Music Since 1900*), a distinction is made between *Gemeinschaftsmusik*—music for the community —and *Gebrauchsmusik*—music written for some special purpose in contradistinction to concert or art music. In recent times, all music written for some particular purpose or for use by any group outside the concert field has come to be referred to as *Gebrauchsmusik*.

proved that by changing their objective, composers could make contact with a very broad audience.

But the third and possibly most significant sign of the new tendency came by way of Russia, principally through the works of the Soviet composer Dmitri Shostakovitch. No doubt the example of Shostakovitch could have been multiplied if the works of other Russian contemporaries had been heard as frequently outside the Soviet Union. It is easy to see how a young composer, living in the midst of social revolution, would have uppermost in his mind the problem of his relationship to his audience. Obviously, the new, untutored mass public was totally unprepared to cope with musical subtleties. And yet the Soviet composer must have known that his works could be directed only to that same mass public.

It is curious to note the effect these circumstances also had on the music of Serge Prokofiev, who spent many years abroad but returned to live in the Soviet Union. Prokofiev may not be the greatest of modern composers, but he is certainly one of the most delightful. His style is fresh, clean-cut, articulate, and was so from the very first. It always comes as a surprise to realize how little the essence of Prokofiev's music changed during two decades, in either emotional scope or technical perfection. Only his orchestration showed an advance over his earlier compositions. One would have guessed that his musical style, so full of melodic invention and *joie de vivre,* would have been just what was needed in the Soviet republics. And one would have guessed right, for as far as can be told from those of his later works that have been heard in the West, his rediscovery of his native land only made him lean more strongly on music of utter simplicity and directness.

But we see the challenge of the unsophisticated audience met most clearly in the music of Shostakovitch. At thirty-five he was the author of operas, ballets, chamber music, numerous film scores, and six symphonies, with more to come. The effectiveness of this music for a large public both inside and outside the Soviet has been proved beyond a doubt. Few people would say that this music is first-rate in quality. But if it seems unnecessarily trite and conventional at times, there is no denying the extraordinary "flair" and sheer musical invention displayed. The man certainly can write music. Interesting from a structural standpoint is his individual use of form, in which the music seems to flow easily instead of being tightly knit together with nothing but thematically apposite material, as is the German custom. The emotional intention of the music is always crystal clear—almost too clear, for one tires quickly of movements that are too flatly one thing or the other: satirical or sober, grandiose or sentimental. Whatever his weaknesses, in Shostakovitch the Soviet Union produced a composer with a pronounced personality of his own, who knows how to freshen the tradition of Borodin and Tchaikovsky so that it appeals not only to the proletarian masses of the Soviets but to the musical public everywhere. His influence seems likely to affect other composers with similar ideals.

1967: The balance sheet of Soviet composition for the quarter century that has passed since the above comments were written reads far more dolefully than we had any reason to expect. What happened? As far as can be judged from the admittedly scarce evidence that reaches us, musical creativity in the U.S.S.R. has been stultified. The revolutionary fervor of the war years, exemplified in the Shostakovitch works of that period, degenerated in the compositions of others into a mere conformism. Prokofiev died in 1953, and Shostakovitch is past sixty (in 1967); by now we ought to know the names of half a dozen younger men capable of carrying forward what these two accomplished. Kabalevsky, Khatchaturian, and Shaporin are solid musical citizens working in familiar idioms, but where are the adventurous youngsters who can hold their own with their counterparts in Western Europe or Japan or America? It is hardly possible to believe that in a country so large and so music-conscious the creative urge has petered out.

During a visit to the Soviet Union in 1960 I heard talk in musical circles of certain younger rebels, practitioners of serial methods or chance music. To effectively "forbid" such composi-

tions, it is sufficient merely to make sure that they are not performed. At any rate, if they do exist, they are not being exported. How then are we to gain a complete picture of the state of Soviet composition today? This is a problem for the Russian cultural authorities to take in hand. They cannot hope to have their young composers play a role in contemporary music unless they are willing to encourage them to face up to the musical realities of our day.*

Dodecaphonic Developments

Now WE MUST RETURN to the early '20s in order to follow the fascinating progress of Arnold Schoenberg and his disciples toward a new kind of musical organization, which came to be known as the twelve-tone system.

A long period of gestation—approximately eight years— preceded the flowering of the dodecaphonic method devised by Schoenberg. The story is told that during the summer of 1922 the composer said to his student Josef Rufer: "I have made a discovery which will assure the supremacy of German music in the world for the next hundred years." Schoenberg had discovered the ground rules of the twelve-tone technique of composition, which was destined to influence the course of music written since that time.

In this second phase of Schoenberg's revolutionary practice, arrived at after years of experimentation, atonality is no longer chaotic, but is systematized and regulated through the agency of the "basic set of twelve tones." † I agree with Willi Reich when he writes that "the recognition of this technique is entirely superfluous to the instinctive understanding of a piece of music so composed." Nevertheless, a brief explanation of Schoenberg's method may be of interest to the general reader, especially since

* In recent months some few pieces have been publicly performed in America by younger composers such as Andrei Volkonsky, Edison Denisov, and Valentian Silvestrov.

† See the letter from Arnold Schoenberg on the origin of the twelve-tone system in Nicolas Slonimsky's *Music Since 1900*.

its basic principles are not difficult to grasp.

Schoenberg's method begins with the twelve half tones of the chromatic scale:

These twelve tones are ordered into a specific arrangement of the composer's choice, called a tone-row or tone series (hence the term "serial" for the procedures of the dodecaphonic method). For example:

This is not necessarily a theme consisting of twelve different tones. It is basically a skeletal framework out of which the composer may evolve as many different versions as his fancy dictates. To simplify, instead of using all twelve tones, let us consider just the first six:

Schoenberg suggests three possible arrangements derived from this basic row, all three based on classical procedures. The first is obtained by reading the row backward, as one would read a sentence backward:

The second derivation treats the row by inversion:

In the third derivation, the inversion of the row is itself read backward:

The series can be transposed in the usual way to any other pitch:

And any note can be sounded in any available octave:

In order to avoid the danger of suggesting normal tonality, two further prohibitions are recommended by Schoenberg. One is to avoid repeating any tone (except for immediate repetition), once it has been left, until all the other eleven tones have been sounded. The other is to avoid doubling any tone at the octave, thus:

since doubling also tends to emphasize the importance of that one tone over the other eleven.

Rhythm is to be left free, dependent solely on the composer's choice. Moreover, and this is essential, the twelve-tone series is to be the controlling factor not only melodically, but also harmonically, thus insuring both horizontal and vertical unity. In other words, the notes may be used to form themes, like this:

or they may be used simultaneously, in whole or in part, to produce intervals or chords:

By the early '30s, Schoenberg was master of this new technique, as demonstrated in such works as the Variations for Orchestra, Opus 31, and the opera *Moses and Aaron*, begun in 1931.

Roger Sessions once summed up Schoenberg's contribution in terms that seem to me to be eminently true: "The truly immense achievement of Schoenberg lies in the fact that his artistic career embodies and summarizes a fundamental musical crisis. More than any other composer he led the crisis to its culmination. He accomplished this by living it through to its furthest implications. But he also found technical means which could enable composers of his own and later generations to seek and find solutions. He opened up a new vein, toward which music has been tending; and the twelve-tone method is in essence the tool through which this vein can be exploited. Its discovery was an historical necessity; had it not been Schoenberg who formulated it, others would have done so, though possibly in a much slower and more laborious manner."

No one would any longer dispute Schoenberg's key role in the developing story of contemporary music since the second decade of our century. And yet, the music he composed within his new system still arouses strong partisan feelings. Some of the difficulty comes, I believe, from the temperament of the man himself, from the depth of that "Germanness" which is said to have been his special pride. Other contemporary artists have been profoundly German by temperament—Mann, Kokoschka, Brecht. But Schoenberg's case is different: an almost desperate fervor, a sometimes painful intensity, makes for a kind of expressivity that is difficult to empathize with, despite the indisputable sincerity and conviction that lies behind the music. Schoenberg's was an Old World spirit; out of an unbounded reverence for past German masters he felt the need of the revolutionary to bring something new to the art he loved. His classicizing tendencies were at variance with his personal temperament, which leaned toward the deeply tortuous expression of sentiment. No wonder it is difficult to summarize the lifework of such a man in a single paragraph!

And yet, when all is said, there remains something profoundly moving in the contemplation of this fiery creative spirit, burning at full intensity. Despite the contradictions of his complex nature, Schoenberg composed indubitable masterpieces—*Pierrot lunaire,* the *Five Orchestral Pieces,* the *Four Orchestral Songs,* the string quartets, and especially the dramatico-musical works, culminating in *Moses and Aaron.* For sheer intellectual-emotional command in the dramatic manipulation of musical materials, Schoenberg had no peer. Twentieth-century music is inconceivable without him.

Schoenberg became famous not only as a composer and theoretician, but also as a teacher of younger composers. His two most renowned students, of course, were Alban Berg and Anton Webern, both of whom remained lifelong friends of their master. Despite their very different temperaments, Berg and Webern shared an unbounded enthusiasm for the ideas and personality of their teacher.

Alban Berg, who died in 1935 at the age of fifty, tended to normalize the Schoenberg idiom by relating it more frankly to its Tristanesque origins. In comparison with Schoenberg's complex personality, Berg's seems warm and sweetly human. His operas *Wozzeck* and *Lulu*, his Violin Concerto and *Lyric Suite* for string quartet are among the most appealing creations in the modern repertoire. Certain pages of these works are of a magical inspiration—sensuously lyrical, violently dramatic, and profoundly erotic by turns. Despite Berg's atonality, his spiritual being had closest association with late 19th-century Romanticism.

Berg suffered from a failing, if it can be called that, which Robert Craft once cleverly named "tonal nostalgia." The composer did not hesitate to choose tone-rows whose successions of notes, as in the Violin Concerto, suggest triadic formations. In effect, this practice negates to a certain extent the antitonal basis of the dodecaphonic method. This trait considerably reduces Berg's historical significance, no doubt, but it does not deprive him of an important place within the hierarchy of latter-day Viennese composers.

The case of Webern is much more complex and problematical. Those of us who first heard his compositions in the '20s recognized, without hesitation, his sensitive and rare musical individuality. Like Berg's, his output was small; moreover, all his most characteristic pieces of that period were astonishingly short. No one then had any inkling of the curious fate that lay in store for Webern's *oeuvre* after he died in 1945. Personally, I doubt whether Webern himself could have suspected the widespread influence his work was to have in our time. I cannot hope to do more than touch upon the main features of the "Webern Case"; it is one of the most fascinating in musical history. Hidden beneath the exquisite sensibility of this Viennese musician was the firm and rigorous spirit of an Austrian schoolmaster. The music he wrote demonstrates his purity of motive, his selfless devotion to a cause, and even more important, his ability to think a problem through to the end with clarity and obstinacy, and with utter disregard for worldly success. All these traits were typical of Webern, and as it turned out, had a profound effect on the development of contemporary music.

The clear and logical thinking of Webern freed him, at least in his own compositions, from any lingering attachment he may have had to traditional methods. In comparison, his teacher and his colleague—Schoenberg and Berg—each still had one foot in the 19th century. Pierre Boulez, with characteristic bluntness, puts it this way: "Schoenberg and Berg belong to the twilight years of the great German romantic tradition, whereas Webern reacted against all traditional forms of musical rhetoric."

Boulez was the first, as far as I know, to point out the weak cornerstone in Schoenberg's carefully constructed edifice of the twelve-tone system. Not only did Schoenberg share with Berg a definite tonal nostalgia; he also poured his new wine into the old bottles of the Classic forms—the rondo, the theme and variations, the minuet, and the gigue, to give but a few examples. Boulez accuses him of having been a kind of musical Kerensky, unable to carry through the full implications of the revolution he himself had instigated. "What then was Schoenberg's ambition," Boulez writes, "once the chromatic synthesis had been established by the tone-row? It was to construct works of the same kind as those of the tonal world he had only just abandoned, in which the new technique of composition would prove its possibilities. But, unless some attempt was made to explore the structures specific to twelve-tone composition, how could this new technique yield any satisfactory results? By structure I mean the growth from given material to the form of a composition. On the whole Schoenberg was not much preoccupied with the problem of forms that would derive from a twelve-tone basis. . . . Webern, on the other hand, succeeded in writing works whose form arises inevitably from the given material."

Here, then, was Webern's triumph. It was he who provided the signpost to the future, insofar as the future is bound up with the twelve-tone method. This reproach concerning Schoenberg's lack of daring in regard to his overall formal structures carries with it still wider implications. Because he continued to use themes and rhythms in the usual way, giving them motivic treatment, his works have the kind of continuity and flow associated in our minds with the tonal music of the past. Moreover, he applied the twelve-tone method only to the control of pitches, vertically and horizontally, other elements being left free of control. Therefore Schoenberg has been pictured as a kind of Moses who could see the promised land, but because of his own 19th-century limitations could not lead music into it. This leadership is precisely what Webern was able to provide.

Webern was the first to write music that is athematic and discontinuous and at the same time under rigorous control. Ernst Krenek calls it "the most complete break with tradition in centuries, perhaps in the entire history of occidental music."

It is not certain, of course, that fifty years hence music lovers will share the enthusiasm of today's young generation of composers for Webern's music. Its historical importance is unquestionable, but its longevity as music is still to be fully tested. His influence may turn out to be far greater than the intrinsic value of his own music, which may some day seem too mannered in style and too limited in scope.

Webern worked with a meticulous hand, but his need to be rigorously logical led him to use specially chosen tone-rows which, when broken into segments, seem to exist in space, as tiny microcosms. This treatment produces a music of detachment and impersonality, an effect which is increased by his considerable demands on the technical powers of the players. The musical line becomes "atomized," and each tone is given its own separate color—the famous *Klangfarbenmelodie* treatment.

Stravinsky, who in his seventies adopted a Webernian technique to his own purposes, speaks of Webern as a kind of saint. Something of the asceticism of a saint hangs over the music. Certainly it is written within one of the most self-restrictive techniques ever invented by a composer. It is partly this control which helps to give Webern's later music a Classic impassivity very different from the Romantic afflatus of that of Berg or Schoenberg, thus indicating the path ahead to the younger generation.

Stravinsky's Conversion

IT WAS not only the younger generation that became enamored of the twelve-tone approach. As has just been mentioned, Stravinsky himself became involved in the dodecaphonic method of composition.

It is hard to imagine two creators in any period more different as men and artists than Schoenberg and Stravinsky: not only are the style and content of their music different; the lives they lived also differed, since one was a teacher and theorist and the other a performer and world citizen. It is curious to note that both men found themselves after the Second World War living in southern California. The crowning irony is that Stravinsky, in the end, should have adopted the method developed by Schoenberg.

It is interesting to speculate on why Stravinsky became interested in the music of Schoenberg and his school at precisely the time he did. From our present vantage point it is quite clear that with the writing of *The Rake's Progress* Stravinsky had reached a culminating point in his own Neoclassic style. It is hard to see how he could have continued along that path. Moreover, Schoenberg, last surviving member of the Viennese triumvirate, died in 1951, the same year that saw the opera produced for the first time. Most important of all was the formidably influential presence in the Stravinsky household of Robert Craft, equally adept in the two worlds of the two composers, and a powerful proselytizer for dodecaphony. The winning over of Stravinsky to a serious consideration of twelve-tone composition was a real coup.

But it did not happen overnight; Stravinsky's biographer, Eric Walter White, points out that "between 1952 and 1957 his serial essays were cautious experiments carried out within a framework of tonal music."

There are few known examples in musical history of a composer turned seventy readjusting his musical thinking to this extent. But Stravinsky, with all the persistence and originality that is typical of him, did gradually make the transition from expanded tonality to atonality. As it turned out, it was Webern rather than Schoenberg who provided the Russian master with the incentive toward the new line. The new technique does satisfy his pleasure in working things out. The twelve tones, unrelated one to another, provide a schema for the concentration of thought and texture that Stravinsky finds so sympathetic. The single-mindedness with which Stravinsky has pursued his muse in these unfamiliar fields has astonished his admirers, especially since the works themselves, as anyone would agree, have not met with the acceptance of his more "Stravinskian" scores.

It is instructive to follow the composer's progress from the strained and somewhat halting religiosity of the *Canticum Sacrum* of 1955 to the elliptical and original *Movements* for piano and orchestra of 1959. One listens and listens again without being certain of having gotten the message. But something about the short ten-minute work convinces; at any rate one is convinced that a new kind of musical communication is being forged. A more recent work of a similar fascination is the Variations for Orchestra composed in memory of his friend Aldous Huxley. Here the orchestral timbres are uniquely fresh. Most of the compositions Stravinsky has writen in his last manner are quite short; an exception is *The Flood,* one of the least successful from a musical and production standpoint of his latter-day works.

It would be foolhardy to attempt a summary of the serial compositions of Stravinsky. They seem to exist in a curious and special ambiance of Stravinsky's own making. They give off a "made" and somewhat awkward quality, but in every measure they bear the mark of the singular individual that is Stravinsky.

＊≫-≫ ✦ ≪-≪＊

2. COMPOSERS IN AMERICA

＊≫-≫ ✦ ≪-≪＊

Composers without a Halo *

→⫸ →⫸ ✦ ⫷← ⫷←

AN UNUSUAL amount of discussion is going on about the music of
the American composer. In fact, it is one of the really live topics
in the musical world today. Some people who hitherto have never
given more than passing thought to American music begin to look
as if they felt they had missed a bus or something. I don't suppose
that the war in Europe is by itself a sufficient reason for the increased interest in native music at this time, but it is undoubtedly
a contributing factor. Also, of course, the recent influx of Europe's
leading composers has helped to focus attention on our own
scene. But essentially the increasing sense we all have that something vital and important is happening right here in our midst in
the field of creative music comes from the fact that there are
many more composers writing, and they are getting many more
performances than ever before. Also, their music is coming in for
considerably more attention in the press than it has enjoyed up to
now.

Music, as everybody knows, has always been the last of the
arts to flower in any country. In its primitive or folk form, there is
nothing more natural to man, but in its cultivated form it seems
to need more coddling than any of its sister arts. Certainly our
own musical history was slow in getting under way. One reason
for that undoubtedly may be found in the elaborate superstructure that is needed before so-called art music can develop properly. You can't have maturity in music until you have produced
all the mechanical impedimenta of the musical world: orchestras,

* Written in the late '30s, this essay reflects a state of mind typical of a
time when interest in American music was on the rise.

opera houses, piano manufacturers, music teachers, concert managers, and so forth. This whole complicated machinery that makes the concert world go round has grown with astonishing rapidity in the last few years. Now we find ourselves leading the nations for sheer number and quality of musical events. To mention but one example—the most obvious one—take the progress we have made in the field of symphonic production. We have today sixteen major symphony orchestras in this country.* It is not generally realized that half of them were not in existence prior to 1918. The consensus is that most of them are the equal of, and several of them are superior to, the best orchestras elsewhere in the world.

If top-notch performances and an active musical life were the only things needed for musical maturity we should by now be at the top of the list of auditory-minded nations. Unfortunately there are large numbers of people, many of them sincere music lovers, who are fooled as to the significance of this showy musical activity. But they must be brought around to understand one thing clearly: first-rate orchestras, brilliant conductors, imported opera singers, child prodigies, and the like cannot by themselves constitute an important musical culture. Don't let anyone tell you that they can. Actually the crux of a mature musical situation is the composer—for it is he who must create the music on which the entire superstructure of the musical world is founded.

Our position today is not so very different from the picture presented by Russia in the past century. Russia's musical culture a hundred years ago depended largely upon the importation of foreign-born artists and foreign music—Italian, German, or French, as the case happened to be. Russia became a mature musical nation, as we have seen, through the gradual emergence of a school of native composers, beginning with Glinka, leading to the Five, and producing in recent times a Stravinsky, a Prokofiev, and a Shostakovitch. This development was important not only for Russia but for all other countries as well. The Russian composer gave expression to a new world of feeling that had

* Twenty-five in 1967.

never before found its voice in music.

The example of Russia, to take only one country, shows clearly that a nation may be said to have come of age, musically speaking, only when it begins to produce composers—original composers. The question now presents itself: what chance have we of producing an original native school of composers?

I have the fond illusion—even though I do not pretend to be an absolutely disinterested onlooker—that it is not mere wishful thinking to prognosticate the emergence of important composers. In the pages that follow the reader will find a discussion of some of the leading candidates in the contemporary American field. That these men happen to be my choice for your attention is less significant than that they symbolize the nascent school of American composers. These, at any rate, are some of the men our musical public must interest themselves in if we are ever to have a mature musical nation.

Not all listeners, however, are lending their ears as they should. Very often I get the impression that audiences seem to think that the endless repetition of a small body of entrenched masterworks is all that is required for a ripe musical culture. As a matter of fact, this continual preoccupation with the embalmed masterwork to the exclusion of any lesser music is one of the outstanding signs of our immaturity. There appears to be an unwritten understanding that our musical public is interested in listening only to the best, the greatest, the finest in music. Nothing less than an immortal masterwork penned by an immortal composer seems to be worth their attention. This assumption is fostered by the attitude, almost unconscious by now, of musical conservatories, radio commentators, recording companies; it is reflected in advertisements of all kinds mentioning music, in programs of "official" concert-giving agencies, in free concerts, and so forth. Being alive seems to relegate the composer automatically to the position of an "also-ran."

Needless to say, I have no quarrel with masterpieces. I think I revere and enjoy them as well as the next fellow. But when they are used, unwittingly perhaps, to stifle contemporary effort in our own country, then I am almost tempted to take the most extreme view and say that we should be better off without them! An example of the kind of thing I have in mind comes from the pen of one of our most influential music critics, a man who prides himself on his honesty and lack of chauvinism in his reviews of native music. Given the occasion, he never fails to remind us that ". . . we in America have no composer of the stature of a Sibelius or a Stravinsky." Well, perhaps he is right—perhaps we have no composer in America who is able to stand up to a Sibelius or a Stravinsky. But what I object to is not the statement of opinion, to which any man has a right, but to the implication that goes with it—namely, that a composer's work has to be "as good as" or "better than" some other composer's work to be worth listening to. I am quite willing to admit that neither Weber nor Mendelssohn was as great a composer as Bach or Beethoven, but nevertheless they both managed to contribute memorable pages to the world's musical literature. And it would certainly seem to follow that, although we may not have a Stravinsky or Sibelius in our midst, we may still be developing composers who are destined to contribute something to the world's music that neither of those two masters can give.

The simple truth is that no composer worthy of the name has ever written anything merely to be "as great as" or "better than" some other composer. He writes in order to say something of his own—to put down some expression of his own private personality. If he succeeds, the results should be listened to by his countrymen even though they may not be "as great as" or "better than" the music of the immortals. At any rate, it is the only way we shall ever have a music of our own.

Geniuses don't grow on little bushes. The great young American composer will not appear suddenly out of the West with an immortal masterpiece under his arm. He will come out of a long line of lesser men—half geniuses perhaps, each one of whom in his own way and with his own qualities, will prepare the way for our mature music.

All I am saying is that each artist of quality has, in any art, a *raison d'être* all his own and that Bach, the master of masters, cannot substitute for his predecessor Buxtehude any more than Stravinsky can substitute for an American composer.

If we are only just out of our teens, musically speaking, there is still much to be said for the charms of adolescence. A certain awkward grace, a quick mind, a daredevil quality—these are the attributes of youth. There may not be maturity in our musical America as yet, but there should be plenty of fun in watching us grow. And instead of harping on our lack of stature by comparison with Sibelius or Stravinsky—or anybody else, for that matter—our writers and critics would do far greater service to their readers by pointing out that in failing to become aware of the growing body of musical creation in their own country they are missing one of the most exciting experiences that the art of music can give them.

New Music in the U.S.A.

❯❯❯-❯❯❯ ✦ ❮❮❮-❮❮❮

CONTEMPORARY MUSIC as an organized movement in the U.S.A. was born at the end of the First World War. The forms of organization taken by the movement resembled those found in various countries of Europe, where they ranged from the local and semi-private concerts of the Schoenberg group in Vienna to the International Society for Contemporary Music, with its many affiliations. By the early '20s the movement had reached New York, and from there it gradually seeped through to the rest of America.

Thus, it has been a comparatively short time since "radical" music began making its way. Yet by the end of the '20s, music that was greeted with snickers and sarcasm on the one hand and enthusiasm on the other had concededly won its place in the sun. A few diehards there may still be who think it has all been a regrettable mistake. But for the most part, even those who were reluctant to allow that composers had broadened the language of music in a manner not to their liking now seek formulas with which to accommodate themselves to the inevitable.

With the introduction of radio broadcasting, the system of the guest conductor, and effective musical organizations, the decade 1920–30 definitely marked the influx of new music into the U.S.A. The performance of works by European and American contemporaries now played an important role in our musical life and aided considerably in making New York one of the principal musical centers of the world. A summation of the accomplishments of these years may present little that is unfamiliar, but it should be of interest from a historical standpoint and to those who are unacquainted with the beginnings of contemporary music in America.

"A group of composers of various nationalities"—an announcement of 1922 reads—"all living in New York City, formed a Guild last year and gave three concerts at the Greenwich Village Theatre." This was the International Composers' Guild, of which Edgard Varèse was musical director. The Guild was founded with a twofold purpose: to give living composers—"innovators" and "pathfinders," as they were then called—the opportunity to have their work performed, and to present the public with auditions of the latest music (by which, of course, experimental music was meant). These two motifs—with variations—have supplied all subsequent societies with their *raison d'être*.

It was characteristic that the first of our modernist societies should have been organized by a European. The Guild was allied with similar organizations in Europe. Varèse stressed the point that the Guild stood for "internationalism" in music. In so doing, he correctly gauged the temper of the time. No mention of the American composer as such can be found in any early prospectus of the Guild. In this respect, only a few years brought a change.

Even those whose purposes are identical often fail to agree on the best means for attaining their ends. The Guild was confronted with this fact at the end of its second season. Several of its members, finding themselves unsympathetic to its methods, determined to group themselves anew, this time as a League of Composers, with Claire Reis as their chairman. The important thing for us to note is that this schism profited public and composer alike, for where there had been one forward-looking group, there were now two.

To these two societies a new generation of American composers turned for support. As a member of that generation I can vouch for our need. What our fate would have been without their help is difficult to visualize. Nevertheless, some idea of the difficulties encountered by composers, no matter how gifted, can be gained from an examination of the ten years prior to 1920.

Performance: the composer of that period was dependent on a local orchestra that occasionally "tried out" the work of a native son, or on a personal acquaintance who was a concert artist. The absence of these openings meant no public performance. Publication: a certain number of American scores were published out of a sense of duty by our largest publishing houses, but these scores were carefully picked from a handful of "official" composers, Edgar Stillman Kelley, Daniel Gregory Mason, Rubin Goldmark, and from "modernists," Horatio Parker, Charles Loeffler, and Henry Hadley. Economic aid: the composer able to devote his entire energies exclusively to composition was practically unknown, for there were few prizes and no stipends or fellowships at the disposal of the creator of music. The careers of men like Charles Griffes, Charles Ives, and Leo Ornstein testify to the dearth of interest in any vital music during these years.

Out of these circumstances arose the American Music Guild (and also the Composers' Music Corporation, a publishing venture headed by Richard Hammond). The generation that was twenty to thirty years old during the years 1910–20—Marion Bauer, Frederick Jacobi, A. Walter Kramer, Harold Morris, Deems Taylor—made common cause. These composers were modest and did not, for the most part, venture so far as public concerts. Their efforts undoubtedly had value for themselves, but they lacked sufficient scope to influence seriously the general trend of music in America.

The influence of the League of Composers and the International Composers' Guild, on the other hand, was widespread. It is a simple matter to trace all later groups with similar aims to the paternity of either one or the other of these two societies. Thus, such organizations as Pro Musica, which made propaganda in the Middle and Far West, the New Music Society of San Francisco, and the Pan-American Association were allied in spirit to the Varèse group, while the Philadelphia Contemporary Music Society, the United States Section of the International Society for Contemporary Music, the Eastman Festival Concerts, the Copland-Sessions Concerts (possibly), and the Yaddo Festivals had closer affiliations with the League.

But it must be remembered that modern-music societies reach

a comparatively small audience. Contemporary music could only find its way to the larger musical public through the agency of the symphony orchestra. For this we needed conductors with vision. It would be illuminating in this connection to compare the programs of Stransky and Damrosch during the years 1912–22 with those of Koussevitzky and Stokowski in 1922–32. The two last-named conductors were held in general esteem, but that did not save them in the early years from being violently attacked for espousing the cause of the "modernists." Other conductors helped to introduce new music to a not-always-willing public: Reiner, Stock, Monteux, Klemperer, Rodzinski, Golschmann, Smallens, Goossens, Mitropoulos. On more than one occasion these men joined forces with the League and the Guild.

All these agencies, working toward a more or less unified goal —that of introducing the music of living composers—were instrumental in developing the latent potentialities of our own composers. The '20s saw the members of the older generation of "young" composers come into their own: Bloch, Carpenter, Gruenberg, Ives, Jacobi, Morris, Ornstein, Riegger, Ruggles, Salzedo, Saminsky, Varèse, Whithorne. At the same time an entirely new generation of composers was fostered: Antheil, Bennett, Berezowsky, Blitzstein, Chanler, Copland, Cowell, Hanson, Harris, McPhee, Moore, Piston, Porter, Rogers, Sessions, Sowerby, Still, Randall Thompson, Virgil Thomson, Wagenaar. The '30s added a whole new phalanx of younger men: Samuel Barber, Paul Bowles, Henry Brant, Israel Citkowitz, Paul Creston, David Diamond, Lehman Engel, Alvin Etler, Bernard Herrmann, Hunter Johnson, Boris Koutzen, Oscar Levant, Robert McBride, Jerome Moross, Earl Robinson, William Schuman, Elie Siegmeister. These men form, for better or worse, the American school of composers of our own day.

Public opinion during these past years has remained comparatively unformed in regard to the relative merits of these composers. We badly need critical works on the failures and achievements of recent composers, based on intimate knowledge of the composers' work. This kind of knowledge few of our critics possess. We may point by way of example to at least one glaring exception to the run of critics—Paul Rosenfeld—who remained consistently and genuinely concerned with the work of our newer composers over a period of twenty-five years. His book *One Hour with American Music* (1929), whatever its faults or qualities, may be said to be the first serious attempt to apply standards of musical excellence to our living composers. More work of this kind must be done if musical values are to emerge from their chaotic state.*

The period 1920–30 re-engendered at least one vital idea, that of mutual cooperation among composers themselves. It definitely marked the end of the Helpless Period. Composers learned to band themselves together and to achieve performances of their works through their own combined efforts.

This principle of action was not being carried out for the first time. Aside from the classic example of similar groups founded by Liszt in Germany and Saint-Saëns in France, there was the precedent of our own Manuscript Society described in the pages of *The Musical Quarterly*. This society functioned at the turn of the century and possessed aims that differed in no essential from those of our "modernist" groups. But unfortunately the Manuscript Society found no effective way of handing on the tradition that it began in our country. Our present-day societies, on the other hand, may proudly point to a numerous progeny who, in their turn, must learn to continue the now-established tradition of organized cooperation among composers.

As in Europe since 1930, modern music in the U.S.A. has entered on a new phase. The struggle that was begun by Varèse and his associates of the International Composers' Guild must be carried on, but on a wider front. By that I mean that new music in future will no longer be confined to the sphere of the special society. Now it must interest the general public through the usual concert channels and the usual interpreters: pianists, singers, chamber organizations, choral societies, and so forth. Their inter-

---

* Wilfrid Mellers published in 1964 the kind of book envisaged here, under the title *Music in a New Found Land*.

est in the contemporary-music field must be awakened, for it no longer contains elements at which they need be frightened.

1967: The preceding paragraph proves how dangerous it is to attempt to predict the course that any current musical development will take. The "usual concert channels" mentioned in it have by now incorporated into the repertoire the radicals of yesterday—Stravinsky, Bartók, Berg, Prokofiev, Milhaud, and even Schoenberg and Webern occasionally—but their counterparts, the Young Turks of today, are as little played as once their elders were. Contrary to my prognostication, most activity concerning new music is still furthered by the "special society," the group organized for that specific purpose. And once again, the unexpected has happened: groups of this kind, which formerly functioned almost exclusively in large urban centers, have now shifted in surprising numbers to the protected province of the college and university campus. Moreover, this is a situation unique to the musical scene in the United States, a situation that is certain to have repercussions in unforeseen ways.

In earlier years the university was known as a citadel of musical conservatism. But now the whole picture has altered; younger composers with adventurous minds have found a home there—a job for themselves, performers for their compositions, and most essential of all, a captive audience. How did this all come about?

An expanding interest in the various arts as cultural disciplines has resulted in the formation of a goodly number of new music departments in centers of higher learning. These benefit from the interest in speculation and experimentation that informs the scientific disciplines. As a result, many music schools within the university complexes now boast composers on their staffs, frequently of an avant-garde persuasion. In more and more schools composers have access to electronic equipment, and more recently, to computer machines for the production of tape music. Moreover, even when composing for conventional instruments, they write a music of such technical complexity that it requires executants with specialized training and skill. Here the foundations have been of considerable help. Small ensembles of perhaps a dozen players, carefully selected for their ability to cope with the contemporary idiom, are subsidized for the purpose of performing the most problematical works. These new ensembles have organized intercollegiate concerts, and several make regular visits to metropolitan centers. Thus an entirely new framework has been set up for the promotion of new music.

Left untouched by these developments, unfortunately, is the "normal" world of music makers and music listeners. How to reach them is the question. The symphony orchestras in America are enmeshed in this dilemma, for they are gradually losing contact with the members of the younger generation of composers, who in turn are bypassing the symphonic medium as an outlet for their creative efforts. The broader the musical base, the greater the tendency to apply a department-store psychology to the choice of works for performance: to sell standard repertoire to the largest possible number of consumers, without regard to the perennial need to refashion our music out of the experiences of our own time. Some modus vivendi will have to be found; if not, our musical organizations will become museums for the preservation of the works of past masters.

Whatever the outcome, I shall not be so foolish a second time as to attempt to predict what new music in the U.S.A. will be like in 1992.

The Ives Case *

⇢⇢ ✦ ⇠⇠

IT WILL BE a long time before we take the full measure of Charles Ives. His career as composer has already taken on a legendary character. The story of Ives is the story of genius in a wasteland. His small-town background, his revolutionary work as composer while heading an insurance firm in downtown New York, his discovery in the early '30s by the younger men, his sudden acclaim by the press in 1940 after the successful performances of his piano sonata *Concord, Mass., 1840–1860*—all this, like the man himself, forms a unique picture in the short history of creative music in America.

It is far from easy to get a rounded view of Ives's gift as composer. For one thing, the man has written much that no one has ever heard. (None of his major works, aside from the Sonata, has been given adequate hearing.) For another, the music that we have seen is so full of technical complexities as to be almost unreadable, let alone playable. But even with our smattering of information concerning his extensive list of works, it seems safe to say that Ives was far more originally gifted than any other member of his generation. At the same time, it seems equally certain that, as Elliott Carter says, ". . . his work . . . falls short of its intentions." Ives had the vision of a true pioneer, but he could not organize his material, particularly in his larger works, so that we come away with a unified impression.†

All this, however, must necessarily remain on a conjectural

* Written in 1933 and first published in *Modern Music* (1934); with some few revisions made in 1940.

† See p. 116 for 1967 comment.

plane until such time as we are vouchsafed first-rate performances of his best work. In the meantime, it is possible to study closely at least one aspect of the composer's many-sided activities—his career as a writer of songs. In that way we may gain some idea of his gift as a whole and the curious position of the composer in the American scene.

In 1922 Charles Ives issued a privately printed collection of one hundred and fourteen songs that he had composed over a period of thirty years. During the first ten years of its existence this unusual volume aroused little or no comment. But apparently this neglect was of only temporary significance, since it is no longer unusual to find the songs on an occasional concert program. To make them available to a larger public many have been reprinted, seven by the Cos Cob Press and thirty-five others (including some new ones) by New Music.

Besides these one hundred and fourteen songs—an achievement in sheer output of which any man might be proud—the original edition contains an essay or, more exactly, a series of loosely connected paragraphs in Ives's characteristically animated, though diffident, style. Here one comes upon several surprising statements. In the first place, we find Mr. Ives apologizing for having published the volume at all. His excuse is that by so doing "a few clear copies could be sent to friends." But later he gives a different reason; ". . . this volume," he says, "is now thrown, so to speak, at the music fraternity, who for this reason will feel free to dodge it on its way—perhaps to the waste basket." At any rate he assures us that from his own standpoint the publication of this stout book containing "plenty of songs which have not been and will not be asked for" is merely a kind of housecleaning. "Various authors have various reasons for bringing out a book. . . . Some have written a book for money; I have not. Some for fame; I have not. Some for love; I have not. Some for kindlings; I have not. I have not written a book for any of these reasons or for all of them together. In fact, gentle borrower, I have not written a book at all—I have merely cleaned house. All that is left is out on the clothes-line. . . ."

Obviously Ives is a modest human being. But he carries modesty to an exaggerated degree, for after having apologized for presenting his fellow citizens with a unique volume of American songs he very nearly manages to apologize for being a composer in the first place—a composer, that is, in the usual sense of the term. Whereas it is true that he did compose these songs, and admits having composed them, he wrote them only "on the side," as it were. Composing to him constitutes only one part of a busy life; as everybody knows, Mr. Ives is a successful man of business. But if we are to believe him, the fact that he composes music does not make him different from other businessmen, for, he says, "every normal man . . . has, in some degree, creative insight, and a . . . desire . . . to express it." This leads him to picture for us a time when every man will be encouraged to be his own Beethoven.

But Mr. Ives is not content to pause there. It is generally assumed among us that the composer who can dedicate his life to the single purpose of musical creation without distraction of any kind is a particularly fortunate creature. Ives has little sympathy for this attitude. He holds that to devote oneself to the business of life is serious, and to devote oneself to writing music while one is in business is serious, but to devote oneself solely to the business of writing music is somehow not serious. It tends to impoverish the artist in the man instead of developing a spiritual sturdiness —a "sturdiness which . . . shows itself in a close union between spiritual life and the ordinary business of life." As one remedy for bringing the merely "professional" composer back into actual contact with reality he suggests that "for every thousand dollar prize a potato field be substituted so that these candidates of Clio can dig a little in real life. . . ."

It would serve little purpose to argue this last point with Mr. Ives. But the question that is of interest is this: why did Ives take so timid an attitude in presenting his songs to the public (since he is certainly not a timid soul either in his music or in his prose style) and why did he choose to glorify the businessman composer as opposed to the so-called professional composer? Let us put off attempting an answer for the moment and examine the songs instead, both for their own sake and for whatever light they may bring to bear on these two questions.

The first impression, on turning to the one hundred and four-teen songs themselves, is bound to be one of confusion. For there is no order here—either of chronology, style, or quality. Almost every kind of song imaginable can be found—delicate lyrics, dramatic poems, sentimental ballads, German, French, and Italian songs, war songs, songs of religious sentiment, street songs, humorous songs, hymn tunes, folk tunes, encore songs; songs adapted from orchestral scores, piano works, and violin sonatas; intimate songs, cowboy songs, and mass songs. Songs of every character and description, songs bristling with dissonances, tone clusters and "elbow chords" next to songs of the most ele-mentary harmonic simplicity. All thrown together helter-skelter, displaying an amazing variety and fecundity of imagination, but without the slightest key or guide for the benefit of the unsuspect-ing recipient of this original edition.

It is self-evident, then, that this publication was not designed to give the musical public a clear conception of Ives's gifts as composer. In fact—and this seems to me to be crucial—Ives ap-parently not only had no public in mind when printing this book but hardly had even the few friends of whom he speaks in mind. The truth is he had only *himself* in mind. For after gathering together the fruits of thirty years' work (which, in effect, literally was a kind of "housecleaning") Ives found himself alone with his songs.

No artist creates for himself alone. To be cut off from the vitalizing contact of an audience, to compose in a vacuum as it were, will of necessity profoundly influence the character of a man's work. Do these songs, then, examined individually, show signs of just such an isolation?

To take the least representative group first: how otherwise can we explain the publication of songs that the composer himself says "have little or no value." He specifically names eight of these; at least fifteen more might easily be added to the list. Most of them were composed in the 1890's and belong to the sentimental, silver-threads-among-the-gold variety. To these may safely be joined about fifteen others, written about the same time, which, if they are not quite worthless, are nevertheless hardly better or worse than hundreds of songs in the same genre by other composers. The songs to French and German texts belong in this group, closely patterned as they are after foreign models. Nevertheless, here in the shadow of Schumann, Massenet, and Brahms, one catches a first glimpse of the later Ives. A somewhat daring middle section, an unexpected close or sharply tinted chord betray the future pioneer.

The first songs of importance date from around 1900. *Where the Eagle* is an excellent example of this group, which includes *Berceuse, I Travelled among Unknown Men,* and *The Children's Hour.* It is only one page in length, but it is remarkable for its depth of feeling, its concision, its originality. Certainly no other American composer at the turn of the century was capable of producing a song of this worth. It is not that these songs reflect no outside influence (that of Hugo Wolf, in particular, is evident), but that the emotional content is authentic; in the rich harmonies and sensuous line of the *Berceuse* or in the charming flow and imagination of *The Children's Hour* one knows oneself to be in the presence of a composer of imagination, a real creator.

The historical significance of Ives as an innovator has been stressed many times. Although the above-named songs are "modern" for their time, they are by no means revolutionary. But what, if not revolutionary, can one call a song like *Walking* (dated 1902)? In imitation of the village church bells heard on a Sunday-morning walk, Ives essayed harmonies that are as daring as, if not more daring than, any written by Debussy and Strauss in the same period. This song plainly demonstrates the origin of much of Ives's venturesomeness; he is a musical realist, a copier of nature. This is further illustrated in songs like *Rough Wind* (1902) and *The Cage* (1906). The latter, with its curious melodic line and its omission of barlines, is obviously meant to suggest the turning about of an animal in its cage. It should be noted, however, that these songs are more successful as experiments than they are as finished artistic productions.

In so brief a summary, one can hardly do more than mention the songs composed around 1908–10 (comparatively undistinguished) or those adapted by the composer from his orchestral and chamber music. To judge these adaptations as songs would be unfair. However, *The Housatonic at Stockbridge* (which originally was a movement in a set of pieces for orchestra) and *At the River* (from the Fourth Violin Sonata) are admirable arrangements of what in the first place must have been cherishable music and remains so in its new garb.

Ives, like no other serious American composer before him, was fascinated by the kind of music that any village band plays. The three "war songs" and the five "street songs" are attempts to incorporate popular material into a serious musical style. His method in several of these songs is to evoke the mood of the past at the beginning with the aid of rather complex harmonies and then to give the popular music in unadulterated form. This mixture of styles is not a happy one; it results in making these the least successful of the songs thus far considered.

But the works on which Ives's reputation as a song composer must eventually rest are the remaining forty or more, that are dated 1919–21.* Taken as a whole, despite many and serious shortcomings, these songs are a unique and memorable contribution to the art of song writing in America, an art that is still in its first youth among us; a contribution that, for richness and depth of emotional content, for broad range and strength of expression, for harmonic and rhythmic originality, will remain a challenge and an inspiration to future generations of American composers.

Where else in American music will you find more sensitiveness or quietude than in a song like *Serenity,* with its subtle syncopations and its instinctive melodic line; where more delicate tone

---

* Many of these songs were composed at an earlier period but were either rewritten or rearranged at the time of publication, which explains the large number bearing the date 1921.

painting than the setting of lines from *Paradise Lost* called *Evening;* where a more rousing or amusing knockout of a song than *Charlie Rutlage,* with its exciting cowboy quotations; where songs to compare with *The Indians,* or *Ann Street* or *Maple Leaves* or *The See'r* or *The New River* (this last containing remarkable Hindemithian premonitions)? There are others, of course, almost as good—*The Swimmers, Two Little Flowers, Like a Sick Eagle, The Greatest Man.* All these are characterized by an essential simplicity—no matter how complex the harmonic or rhythmical materials may be, there is always a directness of emotional appeal and always an unadorned, almost naïve melodic line for the voice.

These qualities are present even in songs that are not successful as a whole. *Walt Whitman,* despite the unforgettably apt setting of the phrase "How is it I extract strength from the beef I eat," remains an unsatisfying fragment, and the deeply moving last page of *Grantchester* does not compensate for the fact that the song as a whole is not sustained. One could add other examples of songs that are mere fragments or are overcomplicated in harmonic texture or deficient in consistency of style.

Weaknesses such as these and others—and it would be foolish to gloss them over—arise from a lack of that kind of self-criticism that only actual performance and public reaction can bring. This indispensable check on the artist Ives never had. A careful examination of these songs will convince the open-minded reader that he lacked neither the talent nor the ability nor the métier nor the integrity of the true artist—but what he most shamefully and tragically lacked was an audience. "Why do you write so much—which no one ever sees?" his friends asked. And we can only echo, "Why, indeed?" and admire the courage and perseverance of the man and the artist.

Little wonder, then, if we find Ives overtimid in presenting the songs to the public for the first time; and little wonder if we find him rationalizing his position of businessman composer until he made it appear to be the only natural role for the artist to assume in America. For Ives had every reason to be timid and to rationalize in a world that had no need for him as an artist.

The small drama that I have pictured here is by no means the drama of Ives alone, but in a larger sense is that of every American composer of serious pretensions. The problem of the audience—not a passive audience but an active one—an audience that *demands* and *rejects* music, that acts as a stimulus and a brake, has never been solved Not every composer deserves such an audience, of course. But for men of the stature of Ives that audience must be found, or American music will never be born.

1967: A gathering crescendo of interest has finally become all-pervasive: the audience has most decidedly discovered the music of Charles Ives. And that audience is more than national; it includes music lovers everywhere. Ives has preempted the place once held by Edward MacDowell as the first truly significant composer of serious music in our country.

I trust no one will object if I give myself a slight pat on the back for having gauged the stature of Ives in 1933. Actually, any interested musician might have perceived it if he had had access to the music itself. But the Ives works were hard to come by during those years. It was Henry Cowell's New Music Edition *that issued the first regularly published work of the composer, in 1929, the second movement of the Fourth Symphony. My own impressions of his music at that time were based partly on that complex second movement, but mostly on an acquaintance with the 114 Songs, which Ives himself had sent me.*

The upsurge of interest on the part of the general music public has come about largely because of the increased number of performances and recordings—especially recordings—of the composer's orchestral and chamber works. In a recent conversation which I had with Nicolas Slonimsky, an early Ives enthusiast and the first conductor of his works abroad, we both puzzled over the reluctance of musicians to cope with the performance difficulties of Ives's scores in earlier days. The consensus at that period was that his music undoubtedly showed the mark of genius, but that it was texturally confused, inextricably complex, and hopelessly impractical for public presentation. How ironic it is to realize that nowadays it is this very "confusion" that makes the Ives music so absorbing to listeners.

I myself was guilty of a similar misapprehension in my 1933 article when I said that Ives "could not organize his material, particularly in his larger works, so that we come away with a unified impression." His complexities don't always add up, but when they do, a richness of experience is suggested that is unobtainable in any other way. For Ives it was a triumph of daring, a gamble with the future that he has miraculously won.

Among the best of the orchestral works recently brought to performance, one must name first the Fourth Symphony, an astonishing conception in every way. But shorter works, such as Decoration Day *(from* Holidays*), the* Harvest Home Chorales, *and the too-little-played First Piano Sonata are unquestionably among the finest works ever created by an American artist.*

Roy Harris *

↦⇥ ✦ ⇤↤

ANYONE WHO FOLLOWS what is written in the press concerning the American composer and American music will surely have noticed a marked reluctance on the part of writers to be specific on the subject. They deal for the most part in generalities—columns full of generalities—but warily avoid naming names of composers or their pieces. Is it possible that the critics are as ill acquainted with the music itself as this would seem to imply? Obviously it is much easier to make broad and unverifiable statements about the state of American music today than it is to come down to actual cases.

One thinks of this in relation to the music of Roy Harris. For if the critics wish to discuss American music—its merits and shortcomings—they should recognize that the work of Harris is one of its principal manifestations; for better or worse, it is part of the mainstream of American music today. In short, this music, instead of vague generalities, is what the critics should be writing about. But I have never seen a single newspaper column that sums up and critically estimates the work of a man who, at the moment at least, is more frequently played, more praised, and more condemned than any other living American composer.

Such treatment is all the more necessary because even among those who know his music well there is wide divergence of opinion in estimating its value. This ability to arouse strong reactions among admirers and detractors alike is a sign of its vitality. For whatever else we may say about it, Harris' music must be set down as vital in today's American scene. It may have no lasting

* Written in 1940.

qualities whatsoever. No matter. It is still significant for us here and now, for it is on music such as this that future American composers will build.

The outstanding thing that sets Harris apart from other composers is the fact that he possesses one of the most pronounced musical personalities of anyone now writing. You can punch that personality full of holes—you can demonstrate to your own satisfaction that the man doesn't know the first thing about composing—but the fact will still remain that his is the most personal note in American music today. Moreover, it was there from the very start of his career. It was clear, despite obvious ineptitudes, in the first orchestral piece he ever wrote—an Andante composed and performed fifteen years ago—and it remains clear today. Harris has grown in many ways. In fact, his capacity for growth has been astonishing. But this growth has been a technical one, giving him more artistic stature because of a greater firmness in the handling of his materials. His essential personality has changed very little in a decade and a half. This is perhaps both a strength and a weakness.

One has been conscious of a persistent attempt to relate the Harris personality to the open prairies and the woolly West—to picture him as a kind of boy pioneer-composer. A considerable legend has grown up around his log-cabin origins and his early life as a backwoodsman. Actually, Harris grew up in a small town in the environs of Los Angeles. It is true that he was born in Lincoln County, Oklahoma, but from the age of five he lived in California. Life there was certainly no different from life in thousands of similar small-town communities throughout the land, except for the orange groves and the cyclorama of surrounding mountains. The corner drugstore, the movie house, the public high school were just about what one might find on Long Island, fifteen miles outside New York. If Harris is a pioneer-composer then we must look for the cause in his blood, or in that of his Scotch-Irish ancestry, rather than in his environment. The proximity of the Californian desert seems to have left little trace in his music. There is practically nothing of the barrenness and loneliness of desert places. It is full, rather, of an urban *Weltschmerz*, of a kind of bourgeois warmth born out of a sense of community with people.

This is not said in any debunking spirit but in order to describe the music as it really is. Personally, I feel its American quality strongly, quite aside from any pioneer trappings. What Harris writes, as a rule, is music of real sweep and breadth, with power and emotional depth such as only a generously built country could produce. It is American in rhythm, especially in the fast parts, with a jerky, nervous quality that is peculiarly our own. It is crude and unabashed at times, with occasional blobs and yawps of sound that Whitman would have approved of. And always it is music that addresses itself to a big public, sure sign of the composer of a big country.

American, too, is his melodic gift, perhaps his most striking characteristic. His music comes nearest to a distinctively native melos of anything yet done, at least in the ambitious forms. Celtic folksongs and Protestant humns are its basis, but they have been completely reworked, lengthened, malleated. These themes of Harris' are generally long and flowing in type—by no means carefully chosen in every phrase or chiseled in general contours. They are likely to start with some ordinary turn of phrase, a phrase that any other composer might have thought not worth considering. But with this as an initial impulse, one never knows when, in the midst of some banal phrase, the heart will be melted. It is their fullness and generosity of feeling that give the Harris melodies their special character. Every piece has melodies in profusion, as if out of his wealth of invention the composer could afford to be spendthrift.

One of Harris' main problems has consisted in the fact that he has not always known what to do with these melodies of his. Normally, melodies are meant to be combined, juxtaposed, developed, elongated—in short, worked into significant forms. At this point in the process of composition, technique comes in; and particularly in the beginning, the adequacy of Harris' technical equipment was questioned. The late start in his musical education was at first held to be responsible for a certain awkwardness, both in manipulating materials and in writing for instruments. But gradually, as though in spite of himself, this awkwardness became part and parcel of his style, taking on a charm of its own. Walter Piston expressed it well when he wrote: "The slightly uncouth awkwardness, the nervous restlessness, Harris would undoubtedly consider defects rather than qualities. If these characteristics are due, as some think, to a lack of technic, let us hope the man can in some way be prevented from acquiring a technic that would rob his musical language of some of its most valuable attributes."

There is no doubt that by now Harris has largely succeeded in smoothing out the angularities of his style—fortunately, without robbing his music of its own special tang. The composer's greatest weakness has proved not an inability to handle the separate phases of musical technique, but an apparent incapacity for shaping a long composition so that the form of the whole is truly logical and inevitable. Harris has not always been of one mind as to just how this was to be done. When he was younger, he was savagely critical of the methods and traditions of established masters. He was intent upon putting his compositions together after processes invented by himself alone. Later on he changed his tactic. He seemed anxious to prove that he was equal to tackling any form that the old masters managed, and the tougher the forms the better he liked them. For a while, no Harris piece was complete without a passacaglia or fugue somewhere during its course, preferably a double or triple fugue for good measure. (All this would provide excellent study for a musical psychologist.) Actually, in neither case did the composer succeed in doing what he apparently was after. Instead the solution was typically Harris-like—in the earlier pieces an inconclusive experimentalism, and in the later works the composer's own peculiar version of age-old forms and technical processes.

This difficulty in handling the formal problem is indicative of a generally insecure critical faculty that shows itself in many ways. Harris finds it harder than most composers to be impersonal in judging his work, particularly while he is still close to it. How else can we explain the tendency on the part of the composer to rewrite each piece after it has been publicly performed before arriving at a definitive version? Or his written analyses of the formal structure of his pieces that seldom correspond to the musical facts as one hears them? Or the overblown "spiritual" explanations that accompany each piece but that, again, seldom correspond to the real inner content?

But these are all minor points in comparison with the absence of critical ability in regard to formal construction that makes so many of his pieces lack a real sense of direction. They seem to be rudderless, heading for nowhere in particular, and as a natural result, ending nowhere in particular. How many times we have heard a Harris movement stop unexpectedly without apparent rhyme or reason. The most glaring recent example was a quartet for strings consisting of four preludes and four fugues. Out of eight endings, seven remained suspended in midair. Or, for another example, take the conclusion of his best work thus far, the Third Symphony. In the version first played the ending was, as usual, unsatisfactory. At a later performance a new ending was tacked on (retained in the published score) that is shocking in its utter conventionality of feeling in comparison with the brave and original section that precedes it.

This is all part of Harris' seeming incapacity for shaping a long composition so that the flow from beginning to end is truly inevitable. To what can we attribute this? Does the composer lack the intellectual grasp needed to mold an amorphous substance like music? Or is it, as seems more likely, an inability to lend himself to whatever exigencies the nature of the music itself may inherently contain?

There would seem to be some curious connection here between the directionless flounderings in Harris' absolute music and his incapacity for adapting himself to any extramusical requirements. I am thinking specifically of his choral works. Harris has shown very little word sense thus far, either in setting poetry according to its natural speech inflections or in mirroring the meanings of words in musical images. His two long *a cappella* choral compositions to Whitman texts, the *Song for Occupations* and the *Symphony for Voices,* produce a somewhat stilted impression, as of something strained and unnatural, in the treatment of the texts, which perhaps might better have been left untreated in the first place. The more recent suite of folksong settings for chorus and orchestra (misnamed a symphony by the composer) is effective as music but shows no real feeling for the individuality of the songs given symphonic investiture. Each of the sharply contrasted tunes is approached from the same angle and given a typical Harris workout. But without knowing the tunes it would be hard to say whether one were listening to the Negro fantasy or a song about a dying cowboy.

Another interesting example of Harris' lack of extramusical imagination was provided by the score he composed for a documentary film concerning rural education among Southern Negroes. What he gave us was a straight chamber-music concert, practically unrelated to the events on the screen. This is all the more strange because his absolute compositions are themselves full of musical drama and, also, because the music *qua* music, in all these instances, produces an impression of strength and beauty similar to that of the composer's best work.

It is characteristic that as a result of this hit-or-miss method some of Harris' best works should be his early ones. The Sonata for Piano (1928) and the Concerto for clarinet, piano, and string quartet (1929) may not be perfected works, but both compositions leave one with the sense that they come out of a real experience. The Harris melos, the emotional breadth and sweep are fully there in these early works. The scherzo movements in both the Sonata and the Concerto are full of zip, entirely personal to the composer. Thoroughly personal, too, is Harris' harmonic sense in all these early compositions. Less commendable are the slow movements of works like the string sextet *Chorale* (1932). These tend toward good old-fashioned sentiment of the unsophisticated, saccharine kind. Perhaps at one time the composer thought that this was typical American sentiment in the Stephen Foster tradition. If so, he was confusing a true simplicity of soul with a sticky form of sentimentality that has its roots in self-pity and self-indulgence. When properly handled, as in the slow movement of his Second Symphony or the *Religion* section of his *Time Suite*, this same basic feeling is conveyed with touching effectiveness.

Among the more recent output, the Quintet for Piano and Strings and the Third Symphony are outstanding. Both works make a powerful impression because of a kind of singing strength they possess. The Quintet is probably the more original of the two, even though the large frame of passacaglia-cadenza-fugue on which it is set up is mechanically worked out in a way that somewhat blurs the total effect. The Third Symphony is less ambitious; but better than any other work of Harris', it succeeds in making a unified impression.

It is the textural content of the Third Symphony that is by far its most original asset. Whereas other composers construct their movements around basic themes, generally short phrases that lend themselves well to metamorphoses of all conceivable kinds, Harris—at least in the opening and pastoral sections of this symphony—builds the music out of a seemingly endless succession of spun-out melodies, which, if not remarkable in themselves, together convey a remarkable impression of inexhaustible profusion of melodic invention. This is seen most clearly perhaps in the pastoral section, where, over a continued background of softly arpeggiated string chords, the solo wind and brass instruments sing separate turns of melody, all related but all different. No other composer would have done it in quite that way. Some of Harris' admirers may miss in this symphony the daring quality, the fighting spirit inherent in the music of his First Symphony (1933). But if the later work bespeaks an acceptance of the more usual conventional symphonic content, it nevertheless shows a marked advance in the grasp of technical problems. One reluctantly accepts the greater conventionality for the sake of a more usable piece of concert music.

Out of this complex personality it is not easy to draw a thoroughly integrated picture or even, perhaps, a well-balanced one.

Whatever one may think, it is useless to wish Harris otherwise than he is. One may show how much better his work might have been. And one can fervently hope that it will continually become more integrated. But there is no gainsaying that, such as it is, with all its faults and qualities, it is enormously important to us in the immediate scene. This is true, above all, because it is music of vitality and personality. Plenty of Americans have learned how to compose properly, and it has done us little good. Here is a man who, perhaps, may not be said to compose properly but who will do us lots of good. We can let posterity concern itself with the eternal aspect of Harris' music, if any. The important thing is that it has something for us here and now.

1967: In rereading my 1940 discussion of Roy Harris' music, I am suddenly aware of a curious dichotomy: Harris the composer has remained very much what he was, but the musical scene around him (and us) has radically altered. For example, my opening objection that commentators were generalizing on the subject of native composers without sufficient familiarity with specific examples of their work no longer holds true. By now, of course, they know a great many American pieces, and certainly they are familiar with Harris' style and many of his works. Also, my prognostication that the California composer was writing music on which "future American composers will build" now strikes me as downright naïve. I had completely lost sight of the fact that a new generation of composers, at a distance of thirty years, would have its own ideas about where a usable past might be found. As it has turned out, the young men of this new crop show no signs of wishing to build on the work of the older American-born composers, the generation of the '20s and '30s. Today's gods live elsewhere.

Where does this leave Harris? Well, he still remains, in my opinion, an imposing figure in the comparatively brief story of our music. He now is the author of nine symphonies. After three decades, the Third Symphony continues to be his most frequently performed composition. But both the Fifth and Seventh Sym-

phonies contain imaginative sections in sufficient number to warrant repertory status. A host of other works composed in recent years testify to the fact that music still flows easily from his pen.

An English critic, not long ago, referred to Harris' "inexhaustible fund of vitality." It is this vitality, it seems to me, that will keep his music alive for future audiences of Americans.

Sessions and Piston

⋙-⋙ ✦ ⋘-⋘

THERE IS every reason to suppose that for a long time to come American music will not show any single profile, in the sense that French music, for example, presents a sharply drawn picture. Our country is too large and too many-sided for that. For instance, in contrast with Roy Harris, the composer from the West, here are two New Englanders—Roger Sessions and Walter Piston. What these men write exemplifies a side of our music untouched by Harris. There is nothing unfinished or uncouth about it. It comes out of a section of the United States that has had from the first a profound feeling for the things of the spirit.

Their common New England background is not the only thing that makes it seem natural to couple the names of Sessions and Piston. (As a matter of fact, Sessions was born in Brooklyn but comes of a family that early settled in Hadley, Massachusetts, where he himself grew up; Piston derives his name from an Italian grandfather called Pistone and was born in Rockland, Maine.) Neither has any quarrel with tradition. They were both, at one time, attracted by the Neoclassic trend in contemporary music. Each is scholarly by nature, and each has spent a lifetime teaching composition at our leading universities: Piston at Harvard and Sessions at Princeton and the University of California, Berkeley. There are other similarities, but it would be wrong to carry these too far, for both men are very much individuals in their own right.

Sessions' music is not very well known. For one thing, by the time he was almost fifty, he had still not composed very much—in fact, he had been reproached many times for the meagerness of

his output. (*Since 1946, however, this is happily no longer true.*)
Then, too, the music that he has composed is more often than not
of a surpassing technical difficulty. This makes it hard to perform
and hard to listen to, particularly for the ordinary concertgoer.
But one must be willing to accept these conditions of his art, so to
speak, or one will never get closer to an appreciation of the music
itself.

Sessions is by nature a perfectionist. Every work signed with
his name is sure to be the result of extraordinary care, perhaps
exaggerated meticulousness. One can be certain that each measure was painstakingly molded and each section dovetailed into
its inevitable groove before the composer was ready to write
"finis." But that does not mean that his music is precious; on the
contrary, it is solid, full-blooded, robust.

More important than mere workmanship, however, is the fact
that this is music of real quality. By that I mean that it is music of
an almost tactile sensibility. If one does not recognize that sensibility one cannot be said to know Sessions' music. For me it is
most evident in his slow movements, such as that of his First
Symphony and the opening section of his Violin Concerto. At
such times Sessions creates without the aid of surface mannerisms
a music profoundly his own: music of an ineffable pessimism—
resigned, unprotesting, inexpressibly sad, and of a deeply human
and nonromantic quality. His faster movements balance this with
a lighter, almost athletic music, brilliant and sometimes dramatic
in character but always flowing onward with a strong sense of
direction. And all his music, slow or fast, is written with the same
consummate technical finish.

More than any other American he has openly aligned himself,
aesthetically, with all those who believe in a universal tradition in
music. He has no patience whatever with easy Americanisms or,
for that matter, chauvinism of any kind. Years of living abroad, of
contact with many of Europe's leading composers, have convinced him that there is no shortcut to an American music; that
furthermore, since we are plainly an extension and continuation
of the European cultural stream, all attempts to avoid the con-

sequences of that inheritance by adoption of a specious Americanism are doomed to failure. This championing of a supranational attitude showed itself, for a time, in the fact that the style of Sessions' work was directly related to the Neoclassic style of Stravinsky. This resemblance has been overstressed by some critics, since it is an influence more of manner than of substance. It is a mark of his character that within this "universality" of expression, he was able to write a music so strong, direct, and tender—and of a special sensibility.

Sesssions' early Piano Sonata was one of the first extended pieces to be written in America in this new aesthetic. It is a solid piece of work—few composers in any country possess the artistic conscience that such finished music implies. The proportions of the whole are peculiarly satisfying, perhaps because of the subtle transitions that connect movement to movement. Sometimes there is a tendency to crowd the page with notes, a failing likely to recur in Sessions. The opening section has disturbed some commentators as being fashioned too closely after the manner of a Chopin nocturne. But to emphasize this superficial resemblance is to miss the purely personal lyricism of the composer. More disturbing, I should say, is a certain lack of true melodic inventiveness, both here and in some of his other works. Instead, we get a sensitively molded line, articulated with all the delicacy and clarity a true artist can give it. But though the composer expends a good deal of mastery on this phase of his art, nothing can quite make up for the absence of a thoroughly spontaneous melodic gift.

In general, Sessions gives the impression of being a philosopher-composer rather than a composer pure and simple. This impression is strengthened by the testimony of works like his String Quartet and the Violin Concerto already mentioned. Music like this is not likely to make friends easily, for it puts extraordinary demands on the listener and the interpreter—even the best-disposed listener and interpreter. Sometimes it seems to me that Sessions writes his music for Titans, forgetting that we are, after all, only mortals with a capacity for lending our attention within definite limits. In his passion for perfection, he either loses sight of or completely disregards audience psychology. It is not a question of giving an audience what it wants, but of *not* giving it more than you can reasonably expect it to be able to digest. It is difficult to set those limits, I know. But one may rightfully question whether the general texture of Sessions' latest work is not too continuously complex, the melodic line too frequently involved, and the proportions of the whole too prone to be gargantuan in scale. More frequent performances of his work would rapidly resolve this question.

A truer evaluation of his stature as a composer in general waits on more frequent hearings of his work. Even as it is, he already enjoys a prodigious reputation in the musical community for sobriety, solidity, all-roundness. With an increase in his productive capacities and a more practical approach to ordinary concert-hall conditions, much can unquestionably be expected from him.

1967: In recent years Sessions has, I am glad to say, been much more productive, and the concert-going public has heard an increasing number of his complex musical compositions. He now is the composer of two operas, Montezuma *and* The Trial of Lucullus, *six symphonies, a piano concerto, a second string quartet, a fifteen-minute Mass, and a long and elaborate work for soprano and orchestra,* The Idyll of Theocritus. *All these were composed after Sessions reached the age of fifty. Something, obviously, released his creative energies, and since he has made no secret of his profound admiration for the dodecaphonic method of Arnold Schoenberg, we may be justified in believing that it was partly this absorption of a new point of view that stimulated his imaginative powers. Whatever the reason, these newer works have added considerable stature to his reputation. There still remains that attribute of his work that the French would call* rébarbatif—*a certain stern, grim, dour aspect, as if the pieces themselves dared you to like them. But it may well turn out that the quality that makes them not easily lovable may be*

*the very quality that makes us return to them always, each time
hoping to crack the nut they represent. In any event, that Roger
Sessions is writing music of serious import and permanent value
cannot be doubted.*

If you had asked visiting foreign composers like Stravinsky
and Hindemith, when first they arrived on these shores, which
American composer they had found to admire, the answer would
very probably have been Walter Piston. This response might be
interpreted in two ways: either the music Piston writes is of so
high a standard in taste and excellence as far to outdistance any
other American's work, or it is couched in an idiom so little
American as to seem quite familiar to the musician from overseas.
There is a certain amount of truth in both these views.

Piston's music, if considered only from a technical viewpoint,
constitutes a challenge to every other American composer. It sets
a level of craftsmanship that is absolutely first-rate in itself and
provides a standard of reference by which every other American's
work may be judged. Piston undertakes no problems that he
cannot solve. Less ambitious in that sense than Sessions, he is
better able to encompass completely whatever task he sets himself. This is important in a musical scene like our own, where not
so very many years ago, mere competence in the execution of his
craft was a crucial problem for each composer. Without men like
Piston, without his ease and ability in the handling of normal
musical materials, we can never have a full-fledged school of
composers in this country.

At the same time, there is nothing especially "American"
about his work. It falls naturally into a category of modern music
that has been well represented both here and abroad since the
introduction of the Neoclassic ideal. Neoclassicism, because of its
internationalist aesthetic, is equally serviceable in any country
anywhere. Piston's frank adoption of the international style makes
his pieces easily negotiable in all countries and therefore quickly
assimilable by the visiting foreigner.

It has been more than usually interesting to follow the gradual growth of this composer. Getting off to a comparatively late start around the age of thirty, he has been consistently adding to his list of works at the rate of about two compositions a year. By now he has amassed a large number of orchestral and chamber-music works. His music has been written entirely with the concert hall in mind, except for a single ballet, *The Incredible Flutist*. With each passing season his work is heard more and more frequently —testimony to the fact that our conductors and performers value Piston's high level of technical proficiency and his direct way of expressing himself.

A typical Piston work is generally in three movements and lasts from fifteen to twenty minutes. His music has a characteristic way of going straight to the point. He knows what he wants to say—and says it, without elaboration. The formal design of each movement is likely to be rather conventional, though worked out, of course, with a sure hand. There is fairly certain to be more than enough counterpoint, since the composer has a special fondness for fugal forms, due, perhaps, to his academic background. Piston's work is most daring, however, in its harmonic aspect. It is this side of his music that is most original, despite the fact that the chords in themselves are by origin rather eclectic; the more astringent and complex harmonic entities have no terrors for him. One can recognize the Piston touch most easily because of his boldness in handling these harmonic textures of every kind.

Among his chamber works my preference goes to the two string quartets. A work like the First String Quartet, with its acidulous opening movement, the poetic mood painting of its second, and its breezy finale, sets a superb standard of taste and of expert string writing. This deft treatment of instruments is patent also in each of his symphonic works. Among these are a Symphony, a Suite, a Prelude and Fugue, and a Concerto. The last-named is a particularly fine example of Piston's orchestral work. The first movement is closest in manner to the 18th-century concerto grosso that was obviously the composer's model. The second is a brilliant tour de force, making use of jazz motifs and reviving a device utilized by Schoenberg in *Pierrot lunaire* and Berg in the *Lyric Suite:* the large *cancrizans* that reaches a central point and then proceeds, note for note, back to its starting point again. Piston carries off this difficult feat with complete ease in the Concerto. The last movement is a passacaglia in form, with an initial theme, stated in the solo tuba, that gradually builds to a resounding climax in the full orchestra. The whole may not constitute a masterpiece, but a good many more pieces of just this caliber are needed to give American music more definite standing in the community.

Needless to say, not all commentators are willing to concede this point. To some, Piston's music represents a new kind of academicism. They find him dry, uninteresting, lacking in emotion. They claim that his Neoclassic manner is no more indigenous than were the Brahmsian pastiches of a former generation. None of these strictures seems valid to me. My chief criticism would be that Piston is not adventurous enough. One would like to know less surely what his next piece will be like. One would like to see him try his hand at types of music completely outside the realm of anything he has attempted thus far. The clear-cut model he has used in the past is good as far as it goes, but it tends to lead to repetitiousness of manner and substance. With his mastery of materials, there is every reason for him to enlarge the scope and significance of his music by broadening its framework. But even if, because of some innate modesty or conservatism, Piston should do no more than add further works similar to those already written, America will still have reason to point with pride to each new piece that he produces.

1967: At this writing, Walter Piston has reached his seventy-fourth year. The steady flow of music from his pen during the past quarter-century has resulted in a body of work remarkable for its consistency of purpose, high level of workmanship, and musical quality. By now he is the composer of eight symphonies, five string quartets, and numerous shorter works for orchestra and for a variety of chamber ensembles. Despite this considerable achievement, I do not find that I have anything significant to add to my previous account of the composer's work. This may be taken as an implied criticism by some, but, on the other hand, such steadiness of artistic purpose and productivity in the shifting scene of contemporary musical life implies a virtue of its own.

Thomson and Blitzstein

No COUNTRY'S MUSICAL LIFE appears to be entirely mature until its composers succeed in creating an indigenous operatic theater. I am not quite sure why this should be so, but I do know that all the history books give it as a special triumph that the English, the French, and the Germans—after the "invention" of opera in Italy—should each, in turn, have developed their own kind of opera. This attitude is no doubt partly to be explained by the fact that you can't very well create a truly national opera without combining the words with a melodic line that really fits—and to have done so properly inevitably means that you have written a kind of music suited to the particular language. In short, there is a close connection between language and tone that makes their successful marriage in dramatic form, with stage incidentals, seem like one of the necessities—and when accomplished, one of the triumphs—of any native musical art.

America is no exception to this general rule. For a long time there existed a strong desire for somebody to write a real American opera. The dozen or more native stage works produced by the Metropolitan Opera Company in as many years left us just about where we were. They all made English sound like "translationese." But now at last we have had two composers—Virgil Thomson and Marc Blitzstein—who seem to have set us on our way toward having our own kind of operatic piece. I am not sure that what they have written is to be called opera, but it certainly is a form of musical drama that is thoroughly absorbing and attacks the primary operatic problem of the natural setting of English to music.

Except for their common interest in the operatic theater, Thomson and Blitzstein were poles apart. Virgil Thomson, the older of the two men, is about as original a personality as America can boast, in or out of the musical field. He comes from the Middle West—Kansas City, Missouri, to be exact; but long residence at Harvard and many years spent in Paris have made a thorough cosmopolite of him. As everyone knows, he leaped into sudden fame in 1934 with the success of his opera *Four Saints in Three Acts*, for which Gertrude Stein supplied the libretto. Since that time his talent as a writer has brought him into national prominence through his musical reviews, devastatingly clever and urbane, which appeared in the New York *Herald Tribune* for a period of fourteen years.

I have always found it difficult to convince my fellow musicians that Thomson is a man to be taken seriously as a composer. They usually adopt the attitude that what he writes may be amusing, but essentially that is all it is. Judged by the standards of the usual type of composer, with his imposing double fugues and triple concertos, I suppose Thomson's work may seem lacking in weightiness. But one must evaluate it not by conventional standards, but in terms of what he himself is trying to accomplish.

Thomson is a man with a thesis. Whether or not his own compositions really come off, his theory about music has validity for all of us. For a long time now, ever since the middle '20s, Thomson has maintained that so-called modern music is much too involved and pretentious in every way. While most composers of the musical left are busily engaged in inventing all sorts of new rhythmic and harmonic devices, intent upon being as original and different as possible, Thomson goes to the opposite extreme and deliberately writes music as ordinary as possible—so ordinary, in fact, that at first hearing it often strikes one as being merely foolish. But even if we agree that the music is sometimes foolish, the idea behind it is not so foolish. This idea is derived from the conviction that modern music has forgotten its audience almost completely, that the purpose of music is not to impress and overwhelm the listener but to entertain and charm him. Thomson seems determined to win adherents through music of an absolute simplicity and directness.

The relationship of this attitude to the Erik Satie aesthetic is, of course, immediately apparent. Thomson would be the first to admit it. But that does not render worthless the point of view or the music written from that point of view. As a matter of fact, Thomson's music does not particularly remind one of Satie's. Aside from an elementary simplicity, it is rather noncommittal in style. It impresses one principally with a feeling of thorough relaxation, with an apparent unconcern about any musical banalities that such relaxation may engender. It is essentially plain and simple music making, in which half the pleasure is derived from the natural, easy flow of the musical line. Thomson has little patience with the Teutonic idea of music as a tightly packed, neatly tied package. He likes a music less relentless in its logic, more free and unpredictable and easy.

There is no doubt that the Thomson theory works best—in his case at any rate—when applied to vocal composition. His chamber works, such as the Violin Sonata and the Second String Quartet, are not quite free from a certain artful sophistication. One can never entirely forget the *parti pris*. And in his relaxed manner he sometimes admits such utterly trifling material—old waltz tunes or *romances sans paroles*—as to make an entire movement seem like a stale joke. Thomson has made use of a great many different types of thematic materials—old hymn tunes, vocal exercises, Gregorian chants, Mozartean phrases, French chansons. Everything goes. When carried off with real flair, the general flow of the music makes one willing to overlook any momentary reminiscences. But by all odds they disturb one least in the vocal works.

This success is due, I feel sure, to Thomson's extraordinary felicity in the handling of the vocal text. His gift for allowing English to sound natural when sung is almost unique among American composers. We can all learn from him in this respect. His uncommonly acute sensitivity to the inner rhythm of English is evident, from the early *Five Phrases from the Song of Solomon* to the later Gertrude Stein songs. That he is no less sensitive to French is evident in his settings of that language, such as Max Jacob's *Stabat mater* and Bossuet's *Funeral Oration*. In all these settings of varied texts, Thomson maintains a remarkably high level of seriousness and rightness of musical feeling. There is never too much music in these songs. It is as if Thomson merely wished to draw a musical frame around the words. This very simplicity of the underlying musical urge is what permits the composer to put all stress on the exact setting of the rhythm of the language. Too much music would seem like an intrusion. Within these comparatively narrow limits in the musical background, one obtains a sense of freedom and variety and naturalness such as is rarely found in vocal settings, particularly in English.

The success of *Four Saints* was due partly to this kind of subtle and natural setting for Miss Stein's by no means simple text. Any other composer would have found the absence of literal meaning in the text a serious stumbling block. But Thomson employed an ingenious device in the handling of this problem: he gave the words their true speech inflections just as if their literal meaning were continuously understandable, while at the same time creating a musical scene that was crystal clear in its emotional intention. The trick lay in making his musical emotion entirely serious and entirely unambiguous in its purpose—practically without regard to the thing said. That is what gave the opera its amusement and charm. One must add also the inverted shock provided by Thomson's antimodernism. Swinging away from whatever might jar or confuse the ear, he wrote with a simplicity unprecedented among contemporary composers, often confining himself to the most rudimentary scales and harmonic progressions. There may be only a minimum of music in *Four Saints*, but out of this music, in combination with the unique costumes and stage setting (by Miss Florine Stettheimer), the all-Negro cast, the melodious prose of the libretto, and the fresh scenic action, an original theater work was created that made all other American musical stage pieces seem dull by comparison.

1967: In recent years Thomson has poured forth an impressive collection of works. Of different sizes and shapes, they are written for all sorts of occasions and combinations of performers. The mere listing of them in the Thomson biography covers twenty-three pages of small print. Among his best-known compositions are the second Stein-Thomson opera, The Mother of Us All, *and the film scores for* Louisiana Story, The River, *and* The Plow That Broke the Plains. *Choral and orchestral works and dozens of songs and* pièces diverses *for solo piano and assorted instruments have also been added to his list of compositions. The production of such a cornucopia-full of music clearly implies a bountiful and purposeful and various gift. I like John Cage's comment: "[Thomson] expresses only those feelings he really has; at the same time"—Cage adds—"his attention does incline to move by means of joy and energy away from an inner emphasis to the outer world of nature, events, and people." One does get the impression that each work is written in a direct and "artless" way, without puzzlement or* arrière-pensée—*almost, I might add, without pretensions. In the end the evidence is conclusive: Virgil Thomson is a unique personality in the recent history of our music.*

Marc Blitzstein's talent as a writer for the stage developed slowly. In the very early part of his career he was something of a problem child. He seemed to have all the requisites for composing—talent, ability, technique—but somehow he had more difficulty than most composers in finding out exactly what he wanted to do. From time to time he wrote works destined for the stage, such as the unproduced ballet *Cain,* an unusually promising piece, and the light one-acter *Triple Sec,* which found production in a musical revue. But these were only incidental in a fairly long list of concert pieces, few of which actually reached the concert hall. The reason was that not many of them really came off in a way that one could thoroughly approve. Either a composition was too obviously derivative, or it tried too hard to be astonishing, or the style adopted was too rigidly abstract. It wasn't until Blitzstein began writing primarily for the stage that he really found himself.

His stage works belong to a category that is better called musical theater than opera. They are meant to be performed not by singers with trained voices, but by actors who can sing after a fashion. Consequently they have a reality as stage drama that opera usually lacks. At the same time there is a loss of the emotional range made possible in opera by the complete exploitation of that most expressive of all instruments, the human voice. As much as Blitzstein sacrificed in giving up the fullness and amplitude of the operatically trained voice he gained in the naturalness and charm of the singing actor. There is little likelihood that one will ever replace the other. I myself should not like to see the musical theater accepted as a substitute for opera. But it certainly brings us closer to a realization of that dream of an American grand opera.

Blitzstein's success as theatrical composer rests on three works: *The Cradle Will Rock, No for an Answer,* and *Regina,* based on Lillian Hellman's play *The Little Foxes.* He wrote, besides, an effective score for a half-hour radio opera called *I've Got the Tune,* scores for some documentary films, and incidental music for several straight dramas. In his work for the musical theater he had the inestimable advantage of being able to write his own texts. (You have to know how very rare good librettos are to appreciate what that means.) Most commentators are agreed that Blitzstein had an unusual flair for dialogue and lyrics but did less well in the construction of a tightly knit dramatic plot.

In his first full-length work for the stage, *The Cradle Will Rock,* Blitzstein was clearly influenced by Kurt Weill and Hanns Eisler. *The Three-Penny Opera* of Weill set the model: spoken dialogue interspersed with recitative and with more formal numbers such as solos, trios, and choruses. There is nothing new in the formula itself, for it is mostly a reversion to a pre-Wagnerian kind of opera—with these differences, however: the subject matter is entirely contemporaneous, the solos and concerted numbers are in the manner of popular songs rather than operatic arias and choruses, and the spoken dialogue and music are more evenly balanced. The whole is something of a cross between social drama, musical revue, and opera. Blitzstein was the first to apply this formula to an American stage work. Some of the tunes that he wrote still show the Weill or Eisler derivation, but they all have their own character—satirical, tender, bitter, or pessimistic. The prosody, which is subtle and complex, nevertheless has all the naturalness of hard-boiled English as sung in a jazz song—an accomplishment in itself. One innovation peculiar to Blitzstein was introduced: the musical sections, instead of being formally set with definite beginnings and endings, seem to start and finish casually, so that one is rarely conscious of where the music begins and the dialogue leaves off, or vice versa. Thus the general flow of the stage action is less likely to be cut up mechanically through the separation of speech and song

Blitzstein brought with him from his experience as a concert composer all the formal discipline of the trained musician. He possessed a passionate love of design. One of the most striking characteristics of *The Cradle* is the extent to which every moment in the piece seems controlled. Nothing is left to chance. Every word in the text appears to have its set place in the dramatic web, just as in music a theme has its set place in the contrapuntal web. I mention this concern with structure with some emphasis because it was obviously one of Blitzstein's principal preoccupations and played a large part in any work he undertook.

No for an Answer is an advance on the first work in every way. For one thing it is closer to straight opera than *The Cradle*—there is more continuous singing. Then, too, the choral sections are enormously exciting. Here the lack of trained voices is least apparent. For once, the chorus seems to know what it is singing about, and this, combined with a directness and surety in the thing said, makes for a completely infectious enthusiasm. But perhaps Blitzstein's outstanding achievement is the fact that for

the first time in a serious stage work he gives musical characterization to the typical American tough guy. Just imagine what it
means to make a taxi driver sing so that the result sounds natural.
In *No for an Answer* the composer has one of the little guys, in
this case a panhandler, sing a song in accents so true as to make
us feel that no one has ever before even attempted the problem
of finding a voice for all those American regular fellows that seem
so much at home everywhere except on the operatic stage. If the
opera had nothing more than this to recommend it, its historical
importance would be considerable.

With *No for an Answer* Blitzstein finally found his own
musical style. You can recognize it in the short, clipped musical
sentences, the uneven phrase lengths, the nervous energy, the
unerring sense of design. There is subtle use of a talky prose
rhythm over a musical background that is very personal to the
composer. His melodic line as a rule, is straightforward, but the
accompaniments may be exceedingly complex, though almost
never obtrusive. Thus, the man in the gallery has a tune to hang
onto, and the more erudite listener has added musical interest
with which to occupy himself. His style, as musical theater, is
always enormously effective, whether the mood is one of heart-
sick yearning or punch-line sarcasm, social uplift or the dregs of
dejection. It is a thoroughly malleable style that can be applied in
the future to almost any subject matter.

This is important in view of the criticism leveled at *The
Cradle Will Rock* and *No for an Answer* because they both are
obviously works with a social message. The old cry of "propaganda" has been raised. I have purposely avoided a discussion of
the so-called propaganda angle of Blitzstein's pieces, because it in
no way invalidates their musical effectiveness, and this is primarily a book about music. But there is this to be said: every
artist has the right to make his art out of an emotion that really
moves him. If Blitzstein, like many other artists in every field, was
moved to expression by the plight of the less privileged in their
struggle for a fuller life, that was entirely his right. If these works
fail in a certain sense, it is not because they are a form of propa-

ganda art but because the propaganda is not couched in terms that make the pieces valid for audiences everywhere. They are not without a certain sectarianism that makes them come off best before a public that doesn't need to be won over to the author's point of view. This limits their circulation as works of art and therefore their effectiveness as propaganda. No doubt, it is not an easy matter to find a satisfactory solution for this knotty problem.

1967: Marc Blitzstein died in 1964. It is saddening to think that he is no longer working at his appointed task. And it is disheartening to realize how little the present generation knows who he was or what he accomplished. Ironically, his present-day fame rests largely on his talent as the translator of the Brecht-Weill Three-Penny Opera.

Anyone who followed the course of his career was bound to admire his courage. One must be almost doggedly foolish to mess with the musical theater in our world. This is especially true of a man like Blitzstein, who began as a child prodigy in Philadelphia, wrote much concert music in his teens and early twenties, and studied with teachers like Scalero, Boulanger, and Schoenberg— only to turn his attention to that most resistant of all media, the musical stage.

In the last two decades of his life, Blitzstein created only one work that held the boards for any length of time, his opera Regina. *In the choral-orchestral field he composed the text and music for two longish works,* Symphony: The Airborne *(composed in London during the war years) and* This Is the Garden, *subtitled* A Cantata of New York, 1956. *Although the Symphony is the more successful of the two, both works are charged with a telling immediacy of musical effect, dissipated on occasion by banalities in the texts. Blitzstein could not resist a certain pleasure in needling his audiences, in telling unpleasant truths straight to their faces. To sing these truths, he thought, gave them even greater point. The moral fervor of these works, when they come off, is irresistible but when they don't, the effect is merely embarrassing. Nevertheless, despite weaknesses, both these cantatas deserve to be heard more often for the qualities they indubitably have.*

In retrospect Regina *must be rated one of Blitzstein's best works and one of the significant 20th-century American operas. Unlike* The Cradle Will Rock, Regina *is a real opera, composed for opera singers, not for singing actors. It has lyrical verve and convincing dramatic impact. The Hubbard family, with whom the story concerns itself, are an unsavory lot, but they provide the composer with an opportunity to demonstrate his gift for musical characterization—sarcastic, parodistic, even derisive if necessary; however, he could also be gentle, touching, and tragic. The work, to my mind, has two main drawbacks. First, although the composer fashioned his own libretto from Lillian Hellman's play, he was unable to overcome entirely the handicap of setting to music what is basically a spoken drama. Second, the injection into the music from time to time of a style derived from musical comedy has a jarring effect in scenes of high seriousness. In short,* Regina *is not without its blemishes, but on the stage the work retains a dramatic force that would seem to guarantee its future, at least in the realm of native opera.*

Marc Blitzstein's life exemplifies a truism that bears restatement today: Every artist has the right to make his art out of an emotion that really moves him. Those of our composers who are moved by the immense terrain of new techniques now seemingly within their grasp would do well to remember that humanity's struggle for a fuller life may be equally valid as a moving force in the history of music.

Composer from Mexico: Carlos Chávez[*]

❧❧ ✦ ❧❧

ONE OF THE strangest consequences of the Second World War has
been the belated discovery that there is music to the south of us.
Why it should have taken a war in Europe to arouse our curiosity
concerning the serious composers of Latin America is hard to say.
An active nucleus of composers has been functioning for some
time in Brazil, Argentina, Mexico, Chile, and Uruguay. There are
signs of nascent groups in Peru, Colombia and Cuba. All portents seem to indicate that we are going to be busy for the next
few years familiarizing ourselves with a host of strange-sounding
names of composers and their compositions. But already two
names stand out as neither strange nor unfamiliar: Heitor Villa-
Lobos, of Brazil, and Carlos Chávez, of Mexico.

The music of Chávez has been known to some of us for more
than a decade. He spent several years during the late '20s living
and working in New York, and his earliest compositions were
performed there at concerts of the International Composers'
Guild. In a sense he belongs with the composers of the United
States, for he owes much to our country, just as Thomson and
Piston owe something to France. The efficacy of the good-
neighbor policy needs no better proof than the music of this
Mexican.

Carlos Chávez is one of the best examples I know of a
thoroughly contemporary composer. His music embodies almost
all the major traits of modern music: the rejection of Germanic
ideals, the objectification of sentiment, the use of folk material in

[*] This chapter first appeared, in somewhat altered form, in the *New Republic*, May 2, 1928.

its relation to nationalism, the intricate rhythms, linear as opposed to vertical writing, the specifically "modern" sound images.
It is music that belongs entirely to our own age. It propounds no
problems, no metaphysics. Chávez' music is extraordinarily
healthy. It is music created not as a substitute for living but as a
manifestation of life. It is clear and clean-sounding, without
shadows or softness. Here is contemporary music if ever there
was any.

Chávez has always manifested an independent spirit in everything that he has done. It is characteristic that from the first he
was unwilling to accept a teacher in harmony or counterpoint. He
read the theory books for himself, compared them critically, re-
examined the truth or falsity of their rules. With the autodidact's
instinct he accepted nothing on hearsay. As a young man
he invented his own simplified version of the conventional sign
for the treble clef—a small point certainly, but indicative of his
independent nature.

Chávez himself feels that he learned to compose principally
by analyzing the works of the classic masters. Using these as
models, he had already, before the age of twenty-one, produced a
considerable number of works. Fully to appreciate his subsequent
development, one must keep in mind the provincial Mexican
musical background from which he emerged. Mexico, when he
was a student, was a country virtually without serious composers
of any importance, without organized orchestras, without even a
musical season. No indigenous tradition of art music existed
there—instead the Mexican musician of serious intentions was
submerged in a German-conservatory atmosphere that was completely devoid of contact with any modern musical currents.
Coming from this unpromising milieu, Chávez succeeded in forg-
ing a music that not only is his own but is recognizably Mexican.
(Later he was to found and direct the only permanently functioning symphonic orchestra that Mexico ever had, and when for a
short time he was head of the Mexican Conservatory, he gave
that musty institution a thorough overhauling. More recently he
was head of the National Institute of Fine Arts.)

One of the most interesting facets of Chávez' work is its Mexican-ness. There was every incentive in modern musical practice to encourage him to use the native tunes as the folklorist composer usually does. Mexico possesses a rich fund of indigenous material in the ritualistic music of the Mexican Indian. Little known even in Mexico, it was difficult to hear and had never been taken seriously by the professional musicians of the country. Chávez had visited the Indians each year, and knew and admired their music even before he himself had consciously thought of it as a possible basis for a typically Mexican music.

In 1921, however, Chávez composed his first Mexican ballet— *The New Fire*. For the first time he had looked away from Europe, turning to sources in his own country for inspiration. In this initial try, Chávez used his Indian themes literally, in much the same way that Falla had used Spanish themes in his ballets. After a three-year period of gestation, he wrote a series of three sonatinas—for violin and piano, cello and piano, and piano solo. The curious thing is that although no Indian melodies are quoted in these sonatinas, they possess a distinctly Mexican flavor. Chávez had managed to digest and rethink the material so that only its essence remained. The piano sonatina is the most characteristic of the group. It is refreshing, original music with a kind of hard charm and distinctive Indo-American doggedness. Here and there perhaps a recognizably native turn of phrase can be discerned, but as a whole the folk element has been replaced by a more subtle sense of national characteristics.

This is an important point in understanding the more mature works of this composer. As Debussy and Ravel reflected the clarity, the delicacy, and the wit of the French spirit without recourse to French folklore, so Chávez had learned to write music that caught the spirit of Mexico—its naïve, stolid, *mestizo* soul. It is a curious fact that he should have been able in his more recent work to alternate and combine the two kinds of nationalism represented, respectively, by the French and Russian schools. Thus, with keen intuition, singlehandedly he has created a tradition that no future Mexican composer can afford to ignore. If

I stress this point it is because I feel that no other composer—not even Béla Bartók or Falla—has succeeded so well in using folk material in its pure form while also solving the problem of its complete amalgamation into an art form.

It is easy to see the difference between these two kinds of treatment by comparing two of the composer's best-known orchestral works, the *Sinfonía India* and the *Sinfonía de Antigona.* Both are unmistakably Chávez, and both are unmistakably Mexican, yet the Indian symphony is a medley of delightful native tunes, whereas the *Antigona* suite is entirely free of any Mexican source material. This same double-barreled trait is characteristic of other pieces that bear the indelible mark of the composer yet at the same time reflect many of the usual modern trends. I am thinking of the symbolic machine-age music at the end of his ballet *HP* (Horse Power), of the piano pieces *Blues* and *Fox,* of the urban popular music in the *Huapango* section of *HP,* and of the re-creations of an imagined Aztec music in the *Xochipilli-Macuilxochitl.* All this music veritably breathes personality, leaving the listener with an impression of absolute clarity and sharpness of outline.

Certain of the Chávez works are perhaps almost too personal. At first or even second hearing, they are likely to seem hermetic and inaccessible to anyone but a Chávez adept like myself. The Piano Sonata (1928), for example, which I have always considered a fine work, thoroughly characteristic of the composer, has rarely been performed. Its four movements are no doubt too continuously taut, too highly condensed for common consumption. It contains a profusion of short melodic germs, none of which is developed in the conventional manner. The piano writing is thin and hard, without lushness of timbre. The general style is contrapuntal, with sudden unexpected mixtures of acid dissonances and bright, clear unisons. There is a certain downrightness about the whole work that seems to imply, "This is how it is, and you can either like it or leave it."

Something of the same quality occurs also in a later work, the Sonata for four horns. It is impossible to imagine a more personal piece of music. There is that same obstinacy of purpose, the same will to write down music exactly as he hears it, without compromising one iota with the public taste. They are superbly Mexican in quality, these pieces, but Mexican-Indian—stoic, stark, and somber, like an Orozco drawing.

It is paradoxical but true that in his own country Chávez is sometimes reproached for not being Mexican enough. This is usually said when his music is contrasted with that of Silvestre Revueltas, whose untimely death robbed Mexico of a very gifted composer. It was Chávez who induced his colleague Revueltas to write his earliest orchestral works, and it was Chávez who gave their premières with his orchestra. Revueltas was the spontaneously inspired type of composer, whose music is colorful, picturesque, and gay. Unfortunately, he never was able to break away from a certain dilettantism that makes even his best compositions suffer from sketchy workmanship. Certain circles in Mexico are anxious to prove that in comparison with the music of Revueltas, with its natural spontaneity, that of Chávez is essentially cold and cerebral. But I see absolutely no need to choose here. It is not a question of Chávez *or* Revueltas, as at one time it was thought to be a question of Wagner *or* Brahms. We can have both men and their music for exactly what each is worth to us. In my own mind there is no doubt whatever that Chávez is the more mature musician in every way.

In recent years, Chávez' activities as conductor and animator of musical life in Mexico have seriously limited his output as composer. A newly completed piano concerto, a long and serious work, would indicate, however, that the composer has no intention of allowing these interruptions to be anything more than temporary. Whatever the future holds in the way of new and unexpected works from his pen, he has already written enough to place him among the very few musicians in the Western Hemisphere who can be described as more than a reflection of Europe. We in the United States, who have long desired musical autonomy, know best what that means. We cannot borrow from so rich a melodic source as Chávez has at hand, perhaps, or lose ourselves in an ancient civilization, but we have been stimulated and instructed, nonetheless, by his example. As for Chávez' work itself, it is becoming more and more generally recognized that here we have one of the first authentic signs of a New World with its own new music.

1967: Now entering his late sixties, Carlos Chávez has discontinued his former activities as animator of Mexico's musical life. He divides his time between composition and guest appearances as conductor and teacher in various parts of the world. His style of composition has changed comparatively little, except that specific national references no longer occur in his music. Their absence makes surprisingly little difference in the overall effect, since the ambiente *remains pure Chávez, nonetheless. One detects an increasingly didactic strain, which takes on two opposing aspects. In certain works he remains what he was—a bold and lucid inventor of new sonorities. His recent* Resonancias, *for example, composed on commission for the opening of the National Archeological Museum in Chapultepec, has nothing of the* pièce d'occasion *about it. Instead, Chávez assaults the ear with sonorities that exploit the extremes of high and low in all the instruments. He is not showing off, he is rather testing his imagination in regard to the sonic possibilities of unusual instrumental combinations and deliberately chosen harmonic tensions. On the other hand, in his symphonies, of which there are four additions (his Third, Fourth, Fifth, and Sixth), a marked classicizing tendency is evident. Long, firmly shaped, tonal melodies propulsively sing themselves out against counterpointed melodies in bass and inner voices. Chávez writes generously; sometimes the sheer welter of notes thrown at the listener without letup or pause (in the Piano Concerto, for example) is simply overwhelming. But then, Chávez has never been a "comfortable" composer; his music has often been strewn with* inconvenientes *for both the listener and the executant. Whatever the style, harsh or mellifluous, it is the music of a personality, one of the most striking of our time.*

Composer from Brooklyn:
An Autobiographical Sketch *

⊰⊰⊰ ✦ ⊱⊱⊱

I WAS BORN on a street in Brooklyn that can only be described as drab. It had none of the garish color of the ghetto, none of the charm of an old New England thoroughfare, or even the rawness of a pioneer street. It was simply drab. It probably resembled most one of the outer districts of lower-middle-class London, except that it was peopled largely by Italians, Irish, and Negroes. I mention it because it was there that I spent the first twenty years of my life. Also, because I am filled with mild wonder each time I realize that a musician was born on that street.

Music was the last thing anyone would have connected with it. In fact, no one had ever connected music with my family or with my street. The idea was entirely original with me. And unfortunately the idea occurred to me seriously only at thirteen or thereabouts—which is rather late for a musician to get started.

I don't mean to give the impression that there was no music whatever in our house. My oldest brother played the violin to my sister's accompaniments, and there were passable performances of potpourris from assorted operas. I also remember a considerable amount of ragtime on top of the piano for lighter moments. But these were casual encounters. No one ever talked music to me or took me to a concert. Music as an art was a discovery I made all by myself.

* In the summer of 1939 the *Magazine of Art* invited me to contribute to a series of autobiographies to be written by half a dozen American composers. This sketch was first published in that year. It is presented here with a few slight revisions.

The idea of becoming a composer seems gradually to have dawned upon me some time around 1916, when I was about fifteen years old. Before that I had taken the usual piano lessons, begun at my own insistence some two years previously. My parents were of the opinion that enough money had been invested in the musical training of the four older children with meager results and had no intention of squandering further funds on me. But despite the reasonableness of this argument, my persistence finally won them over. I distinctly remember with what fear and trembling I knocked on the door of Mr. Leopold Wolfsohn's piano studio on Clinton Avenue in Brooklyn, and—once again all by myself—arranged for piano lessons.

The idea of composing came, as I say, several years later. It was Mr. Wolfsohn who helped me find a harmony teacher when I realized that to be a composer one had to study harmony. At first I had imagined that harmony could be learned by correspondence course, but a few trial lessons cured me of that illusion. So it came about that in the fall of 1917 I began harmony lessons with the late Rubin Goldmark. My new teacher was a nephew of Karl Goldmark, the famous composer of *The Queen of Sheba*. Goldmark had an excellent grasp of the fundamentals of music and knew very well how to impart his ideas. This was a stroke of luck for me. I was spared the flounderings that so many American musicians have suffered through incompetent teaching at the start of their theoretical training.

By the spring of 1918 I had been graduated from high school and was able to devote all my energies to music. It seems curious now that public school played so small a part in my musical training. I neither sang in the school chorus nor played in the school orchestra. Music classes were a kind of joke—we were not even taught to sight-read a single vocal line properly. Perhaps things have changed for the better in that respect. A young person with musical aptitudes would probably find more scope in the regular school curriculum for his or her talents nowadays.

During these formative years I had been gradually uncovering for myself the literature of music. Some instinct seemed to lead me logically from Chopin's waltzes to Haydn's sonatinas to Beethoven's sonatas to Wagner's operas. And from there it was but a step to Hugo Wolf's songs, to Debussy's preludes, and to Scriabin's piano poems. In retrospect it all seems surprisingly orderly. As far as I can remember no one ever told me about "modern music." I apparently happened on it in the natural course of my musical explorations. It was Goldmark, a convinced conservative in musical matters, who first actively discouraged this commerce with the "moderns." That was enough to whet any young man's appetite. The fact that the music was in some sense forbidden only increased its attractiveness. Moreover, it was difficult to get. The war had made the importation of new music a luxury; Scriabin and Debussy and Ravel were bringing high prices. By the time I was eighteen I already had something of the reputation of a musical rebel—in Goldmark's eyes at any rate.

As might be expected, my compositions of that period, mostly two-page songs and piano pieces, began to show traces of my musical enthusiasms. It soon was clear that Goldmark derived no pleasure from seeing what seemed to him to be "modernistic experiments." The climax came when I brought for his critical approval a piano piece called *The Cat and the Mouse*. He regretfully admitted that he had no criteria by which to judge such music. From that time on my compositional work was divided into two compartments: the pieces that really interested me, that were composed on the side, so to speak, and the conventional student work written in conformity with the "rules."

During these student years I missed very much the companionship of other music students. I had a sense of isolation and of working too much by myself. In America today there are undoubtedly other young musicians who are isolated in big and small communities in a similar fashion.

It was a foregone conclusion around 1920 that anyone who had serious pretensions as a composer would have to go abroad to finish his studies. Before the war it was taken for granted that "abroad" for composers meant Germany. But I belonged to the postwar generation, and so for me "abroad" inevitably meant

Paris. The hitch was that I knew not a living soul in Paris—or in all France, for that matter.

At about that time, I read in a musical journal of the proposed establishment of a music school for Americans to be inaugurated during the summer of 1921 in the Palace at Fontainebleau. I was so quick to respond to this announcement that my name headed the list of enrollments. My plan was to stay on in Paris for the winter after the closing of summer school. This would give me a chance to acclimatize myself to French ways and at the same time to find a suitable teacher with whom to continue my studies.

Paul Vidal of the Paris Conservatory taught us composition at the Fontainebleau School. He turned out to be a French version of Rubin Goldmark, except that he was harder to understand because of the peculiar French *patois* that he talked. Before the summer was very far advanced, rumors began to circulate of the presence at school of a brilliant harmony teacher, a certain Nadia Boulanger. This news naturally had little interest for me, since I had long finished *my* harmonic studies. It took a considerable amount of persuasion on the part of a fellow student before I consented to "look in" on Mlle. Boulanger's class. On that particular day she was explaining the harmonic structure of one of the scenes from *Boris Godunov*. I had never before witnessed such enthusiasm and such clarity in teaching. I immediately suspected that I had found my teacher.

There were several mental hurdles to get over first, however. No one to my knowledge had ever before thought of studying composition with a woman. This idea was absurd on the face of it. Everyone knows that the world has never produced a first-rate woman composer, so it follows that no woman could possibly hope to teach composition. Moreover, how would it sound to the folks back home? The whole idea was just a bit too revolutionary.

Nevertheless, and despite these excellent reasons, I visited Mlle. Boulanger in the fall and asked her to accept me as her pupil. She must have been about thirty-three years old at that time, and as far as I know, I was her first full-fledged American composition student. I mention this with a certain amount of understandable pride in view of the large number of young American composers who have followed, and are still following, in my footsteps. Two qualities possessed by Mlle. Boulanger make her unique: one is her consuming love for music, and the other is her ability to inspire a pupil with confidence in his own creative powers. Add to this an encyclopedic knowledge of every phase of music past and present, an amazing critical perspicacity, and a full measure of feminine charm and wit. The influence of this remarkable woman on American creative music will some day be written in full.

My one year in Paris was stretched to two and then to three years. It was a fortunate time to be studying music in France. All the pent-up energies of the war years were unloosed. Paris was an international proving ground for all the newest tendencies in music. Much of the music that had been written during the dark years of the war was now being heard for the first time. Schoenberg, Stravinsky, Bartók, Falla were all new names to me. And the younger generation was heard from also—Milhaud, Honegger, Auric, and the other noisy members of the Group of Six. Works by many composers outside France were performed —Hindemith, Prokofiev, Szymanowski, Malipiero, Kodály. It was a rarely stimulating atmosphere in which to carry on one's studies.

Many of these new works were given their première at the Concerts Koussevitzky. Every spring and fall Serge Koussevitzky organized and conducted a series of orchestral concerts at the Paris Opera, where a feast of new compositions was offered. I attended these concerts regularly for three years with my friend and roommate Harold Clurman (later to become director of the Group Theatre in New York). The watchword in those days was "originality." The laws of rhythm, of harmony, of construction had all been torn down. Every composer in the vanguard set out to remake these laws according to his own conceptions. And I suppose that I was no exception despite my youth—or possibly because of it.

During my three years in Paris I had composed several Motets for unaccompanied voices, a Passacaglia for piano, a song for soprano with the accompaniment of flute and clarinet, a Rondino for string quartet, and finally a one-act ballet called *Grohg*, my first essay in the orchestral field. With this baggage under my arm I returned to America in June, 1924.

Looking backward to that time, I am rather amazed at my own ignorance of musical conditions in America. I mean, of course, conditions as they affected composers. How a composer managed to get his compositions performed or published and how he was expected to earn his living were equally mysterious. I had left my drab Brooklyn street as a mere student with practically no musical connections. I was returning there in much the same state. As far as I was concerned, America was virgin soil.

The immediate business in hand, however, was the writing of a symphony for organ and orchestra. Nadia Boulanger had been engaged to appear as organ soloist with the old New York Symphony and the Boston Symphony the following winter. Before I left Paris she had had the courage to ask me to supply her with an organ concerto for her American tour. I, on the other hand, had had the temerity to accept the invitation. This, despite the fact that I had written only one work in extended form before then, that I had only a passing acquaintance with the organ as an instrument, and that I had never heard a note of my own orchestration. The symphony was composed that summer while I perfunctorily performed my duties as pianist in a hotel trio at Milford, Pennsylvania.

I returned to New York in the fall to finish the orchestration of the symphony and began to look about me. Without my being aware of it, postwar activities in Europe had affected American musical circles also. Shortly after my departure for France the International Composers' Guild and the League of Composers had begun to familiarize the American public with the output of the new composers of the "left." Like many other composers of so-called radical tendencies, I naturally turned to them for support. Through the good offices of Marion Bauer I was invited to play some of my works for the executive board of the League of Composers. The board voted to accept my two piano pieces—*The Cat and the Mouse* and the Passacaglia—for performance at their November concert. This was the first performance of any of my compositions in my native land. It was followed in January by the performance of the Symphony for organ and orchestra, with Walter Damrosch as conductor and Nadia Boulanger as soloist.

An unexpected incident occurred at this concert, indicative of the attitude toward "modern music" at that period. When the performance of my symphony was over and the audience had settled itself for the next number on the program, Dr. Damrosch turned round and addressed his public as follows: "If a young man at the age of twenty-three can write a symphony like that, in five years he will be ready to commit murder." Fearing that the elderly ladies in his audience had been shocked by the asperities of the new style in music, Dr. Damrosch found this way of consoling them. That, at any rate, was my interpretation of his little speech. In any event, his prophecy luckily came to nothing.

The performance of the symphony brought me into personal contact with the conductor whose concerts I had admired in Paris. Serge Koussevitzky was serving his first term as conductor of the Boston Symphony that winter. Here was a stroke of extraordinary good fortune for me and for American music generally. For Koussevitzky brought with him from Paris not only his conductorial prowess but also his passion for encouraging whatever he felt to be new and vital in contemporary music. Throughout his long tenure in Boston he consistently championed young American music while continuing to introduce novelties from Europe. We Americans are all in his debt.

Koussevitzky made no secret of his liking for my symphony. He told me that he had agreed to conduct a chamber orchestra in an all-modern concert for the League of Composers the following winter. It was his idea, agreed to by the League, that I be commissioned to write a new work for that concert. It seemed to me that my first winter in America was turning out better than I had had reason to expect.

But one rather important item was being neglected—my financial setup. For lack of a better solution I had decided to make a living by teaching. In the fall I had opened a studio on West Seventy-fourth Street in Manhattan and sent out the usual announcements. Unfortunately the effect of this move was nil. It produced not one pupil. By the time the Symphony had been played in Boston the situation was acute. Something had to be done. It was Paul Rosenfeld who came to the rescue. While still a student in Brooklyn, I had read his appreciations of contemporary music in the *Dial*. The morning after the performance of the piano pieces at the League concert, he called me up to tell me how much he liked them. (I couldn't have been more surprised if President Coolidge had telephoned me.) It was 1924; money was plentiful and art patrons were numerous. Through a mutual friend Rosenfeld was asked if he could not find a musical Maecenas to come to the aid of an indigent young composer. Rosenfeld said he could, and did. Shortly afterward, the Guggenheim Memorial Foundation was established for a preliminary trial year, and I was awarded the first fellowship extended to a composer. This was renewed the following year, and so financial stability was assured until the fall of 1927.

Now I was free to devote my entire energies to the composition of the new work for Koussevitzky's League concert. I was anxious to write a work that would immediately be recognized as American in character. This desire to be "American" was symptomatic of the period. It made me think of my Symphony as too European in inspiration. I had experimented a little with the rhythms of popular music in several earlier compositions, but now I wanted frankly to adopt the jazz idiom and see what I could do with it in a symphonic way. Rosenfeld suggested the MacDowell Colony as a good place to work during the summer months. It was there that I wrote my *Music for the Theatre*, a suite in five parts for small orchestra.

It was also at the MacDowell Colony that I made the

acquaintance of another young American composer in embryo, Roy Harris. I already knew Virgil Thomson and Douglas Moore from my Paris days, and shortly after meeting Harris I came to know Roger Sessions, Walter Piston, and Carlos Chávez. These contacts with kindred spirits among fellow composers led me to take an active interest in the welfare of American composers in general. The first problem to be attacked was the matter of performance. We thought that American compositions were not being performed enough. (They are still not performed enough, it seems to me.) With Roger Sessions I organized a series of concerts, under the name of the Copland-Sessions Concerts, which functioned from 1928 to 1931. American music made up the bulk of our programs—that was our one innovation. Later I was active in organizing several festivals of American music at Yaddo, in Saratoga Springs, New York. These proved to be the first of a series of efforts toward the improvement of the economic and artistic status of the American composer.

The jazz element in *Music for the Theatre* was further developed in my next work, a Concerto for Piano and Orchestra, which I played as soloist with the Boston Symphony in Boston and New York. This proved to be the last of my "experiments" with symphonic jazz. With the Concerto I felt I had done all I could with the idiom, considering its limited emotional scope. True, it was an easy way to be American in musical terms, but all American music could not possibly be confined to two dominant jazz moods—the blues and the snappy number. The characteristic rhythmic element of jazz, being independent of mood, yet purely indigenous, will undoubtedly continue to be used in serious native music.

In 1929, just before the economic crash, the RCA Victor Company offered an award of $25,000 for a symphonic work. This unprecedented sum obviously implied a composition of major proportions. With this in mind, I began work on a big one-movement symphony that I planned to submit for the prize under the title *Symphonic Ode*. Unfortunately, two weeks before the competition was to close officially, I realized that I could not finish my *Ode* in time. In despair at having nothing to offer, I seized upon the old ballet *Grohg,* written in Paris, and extracting three of the movements I liked best, called the whole a *Dance Symphony* and sent it in on the final day. The judges found no one work worthy of the full award and so decided to divide it among five of the contestants. My *Dance Symphony* won me $5,000. The *Symphonic Ode* was finished subsequently and performed as one of the works celebrating the fiftieth anniversary of the Boston Symphony.

In retrospect it seems to me that the *Ode* marks the end of a certain period in my development as a composer. The works that follow it are no longer so grandly conceived. The *Piano Variations* (1930), the *Short Symphony* (1933), the *Statements* for orchestra (1935) are more spare in sonority, more lean in texture. They are still comparatively difficult to perform and difficult for an audience to comprehend.

During the mid-'30s I began to feel an increasing dissatisfaction with the relations of the music-loving public and the living composer. The old "special" public of the modern-music concerts had fallen away, and the conventional concert public continued apathetic or indifferent to anything but the established classics. It seemed to me that we composers were in danger of working in a vacuum. Moreover, an entirely new public for music had grown up around the radio and phonograph. It made no sense to ignore them and to continue writing as if they did not exist. I felt that it was worth the effort to see if I couldn't say what I had to say in the simplest possible terms.

My most recent works, in their separate ways, embody this tendency toward an imposed simplicity. *El Salón México* is an orchestral work based on Mexican tunes; *The Second Hurricane* is an opera for school children of high-school age to perform; *Music for Radio* was written on a commission from the Columbia Broadcasting Company especially for performance on the air; *Billy the Kid,* a ballet written for the Ballet Caravan, utilizes simple cowboy songs as melodic material; *The City, Of Mice and Men,* and *Our Town* are scores for the films. The reception accorded these works in the last two or three years encourages me to believe that the American composer is destined to play a more commanding role in the musical future of his own country.

1967: The preceding pages were written a good many years ago. In the intervening period I have learned, to my discomfiture, that the writing of an autobiographical sketch in mid-career is fraught with peril. Commentators, pleased to be able to quote literally, are convinced that they have pinned the composer down for all time. The statements quoted may be long out of date, but the quotation marks that surround them make them seemingly unassailable. Thus, the final two paragraphs of my brief memoir have done me considerable harm. The assertion that I wished "to see if I couldn't say what I had to say in the simplest possible terms" and the mention of "an imposed simplicity" were taken to mean that I had renounced my more complex and "difficult" music, turned my back on the cultivated audience that understands a sophisticated musical language, and henceforth would write music solely for the "masses." Quoted and requoted, these remarks of mine emphasized a point of view which, although apposite at the time of writing—the end of the '30s—seems to me to constitute an oversimplification of my aims and intentions, especially when applied to a consideration of my subsequent work and of my work as a whole.

Taken in context, my position at that time is not too surprising. By the end of 1939, the artists of America had lived through a very special ten years, aptly named "the fervent years" in Harold Clurman's perceptive phrase. In all the arts the Depression had aroused a wave of sympathy for and identification with the plight of the common man. In music this was combined with the heady wine of suddenly feeling ourselves—the composers, that is —needed as never before. Previously our works had been largely self-engendered: no one asked for them; we simply wrote them out of our own need. Now, suddenly, functional music was in demand as never before, certainly as never before in the experience of our serious composers. Motion-picture and ballet companies, radio stations and schools, film and theater producers discovered us. The music appropriate for the different kinds of cooperative ventures undertaken by these people had to be simpler and more direct. There was a "market" especially for music evocative of the American scene—industrial backgrounds, landscapes of the Far West, and so forth. This kind of role for music, so new then, is now taken for granted by both entrepreneurs and composers. But in the late '30s and early '40s it was almost without precedent, and moreover, it developed at just the time when the economic pinch of the Depression had really reached us. No wonder we were pleased to find ourselves sought after and were ready to compose in a manner that would satisfy both our collaborators and ourselves.

Even our own government needed us. For the first time the State Department sponsored official visits of American creative artists and performers to foreign countries. In 1941 the Office of the Coordinator of Inter-American Affairs, under the chairmanship of Nelson Rockefeller, invited me to participate in our good-neighbor policy by going to South America for several months. I had acquired some sense of the Latin-American temperament and a fair smattering of Spanish during several visits to Mexico in the '30s. Carlos Chávez in 1932 had sponsored my first visit south of the border with the tempting bait of an all-Copland program for the first time anywhere. But my initial contact in 1941 with the music and culture of seven different South American countries (to which were added Mexico on the way down and Cuba on the way back) was an eye-opener. I met and talked with almost sixty composers, listened to many of their works, and played and discussed with them recent compositions by their North American confreres. In many ways we found our situation and problems to be similar, especially vis-à-vis Europe; our slow development toward musical independence was paralleled by their own experience. This resemblance created a strong bond between us—a bond we both sensed, and one that still attaches me to my South American composer friends. It was further cemented in later years when numbers of the most gifted younger Latin-American musicians came to study at Tanglewood.

I associate this first trip to South America with the completion of my Piano Sonata in Santiago de Chile, during their September national holidays. One month later I gave the work its first public performance in Buenos Aires at a concert sponsored by La Nueva Musica, an organization with aims not unlike those of our own League of Composers. The Piano Sonata is a piece of absolute music, written without conscious reference to any folk origins. This is also true of my Sonata for Violin and Piano, completed two years later, and of my Third Symphony, completed in 1946. *Appalachian Spring* also dates from these years (1944); it is generally thought to be folk inspired, despite the fact that the Shaker tune *'Tis the Gift to Be Simple* is the only actual folk tune quoted. I stress this point because of the mistaken notion that my music of this period is larded with native musical materials. A confusion seems to exist between rhythms and melodies that suggest a certain American *ambiente*, often arrived at unconsciously, and specific folk themes, such as those which in my ballets *Billy the Kid* and *Rodeo* are utilized and developed in a way that I like to think is my own.

Most of *Appalachian Spring* and a good part of my Violin Sonata were composed at night at the Samuel Goldwyn Studios in Hollywood. An air of mystery hovers over a film studio after dark. Its silent and empty streets give off something of the atmosphere of a walled medieval town; no one gets in or out without passing muster with the guards at the gates. This seclusion provided the required calm for evoking the peaceful, open countryside of rural Pennsylvania depicted in *Appalachian Spring*.

During this time Groucho Marx was employed by Mr. Goldwyn, and I used to see him occasionally in the studio lunchroom, where we exchanged pleasantries. One night I was genuinely surprised to come upon him at a concert of modern music in downtown Los Angeles where my Piano Sonata was being given a local première. "Whatever you do," I said with a smile, "don't tell Mr. Goldwyn about this advanced stuff I write, or you might frighten him. After all," I added jokingly, "I have a split personality."

Groucho came right back with, "Well, it's O.K., as long as you split it with Mr. Goldwyn."

Appalachian Spring owes its origin to the fact that in 1942 the well-known music patron Mrs. Elizabeth Sprague Coolidge was taken to a performance of Martha Graham's Dance Company. Stimulated by what she saw, Mrs. Coolidge, with typical generosity, decided to commission three composers of Miss Graham's choice to compose ballets for her. Martha chose Hindemith, Milhaud, and myself. I have since felt that the music I wrote was tailored to the special talents and very special personality of Miss Graham. The ballet took me about a year to complete. I remember thinking at the time: "How foolhardy it is to be spending all this time writing a thirty-five-minute score for a modern-dance company, knowing how short-lived most ballets *and* their scores are." But as sometimes happens, this musical composition took on a fate of its own, quite different from the expectation of its creator. The Suite I derived from the ballet, transcribed for symphony orchestra (the original instrumentation was for thirteen players), won me two well-known prizes and did much to bring my name before a wider public.

During the '40s I began to give talks in various parts of the country about contemporary music and contemporary American music. One of these engagements took me to the Chicago Musical College in the spring of 1946. I recall the visit partly because of a telephone conversation I had with the manager of the touring Cincinnati Symphony. He explained that the conductor, Eugene Goossens, had suddenly fallen ill, and since the Chicago program included the Suite from *Appalachian Spring* he wished to know whether I would be willing to substitute as conductor of my own composition. The proposal was most inviting, but the cold fact was that I had only very sporadically conducted any kind of orchestra, and besides, I didn't know *Appalachian Spring* from the conductor's standpoint; so I was reluctantly forced to reply, "Sorry, but I can't do it."

I date from that episode a determination to learn how to conduct at least my own works. After all, every composer secretly thinks he knows best how his own music should sound. Moreover, I had reason to believe I was something of a performer by nature. I knew that I liked audiences and they seemed to respond to me. But the question was, how do you practice conducting without an orchestra to practice on?

An unexpected solution presented itself in 1947 when I was asked to tour Latin America for the second time. Carlos Chávez invited me to conduct his Orquesta Sinfónica de México in my Third Symphony, and similar opportunities were given me in Montevideo and Buenos Aires. Here was a chance for working out problems away from home, in places where I might expect to enjoy all the advantages of a visiting fireman. Encouraged by the reaction of orchestras and audiences on that tour, I intermittently continued similar "practice" in subsequent years in far-off places like Rome, Trieste, Zurich, London, Paris, Munich—anywhere, as is evident, except the United States.

Finally I felt ready to face an American audience. This time when the telephone rang (in 1956), it was the manager of the Chicago Symphony who was calling, to invite me to conduct the orchestra at Ravinia Park, and I was able to say, delightedly, "Of course, yes!" The concert must have gone off well enough if I can judge by the number of times I was invited back in successive years.

An elderly and wise woman once gave me some excellent advice. "Aaron," she said, "it is very important, as you get older, to engage in an activity that you didn't engage in when you were young, so that you are not continually in competition with yourself as a young man." The conductor's baton was my answer to that problem. Conducting, as everyone knows, is a bug—once you are bitten it is the very devil to get rid of. What makes it worse is the fact that you get better at it all the time—more expert in rehearsing, more economical in gesture, more relaxed in actual performance. By now I have worked with more than fifty symphonic organizations in countries around the world. Sometimes I think my best audiences have been in England and Scotland, where repeated concert appearances and exposure on BBC television and radio have forged a bond that I know will be lasting from my side and I hope will be lasting from theirs.

One of my fondest memories of this late-starting career is associated with Charles Munch and the Boston Symphony Orchestra. Mr. Munch invited me along as guest conductor when the Boston Symphony made its first visit to Japan, the Philippines, and Australia in 1960. I led the orchestra in Osaka, Yawata, Okayama, Shizuoka, Koriyama, Nagaoka, and of course, Tokyo. On nights when Mr. Munch conducted I watched with fascination the impassive faces of Japanese audiences while a Tchaikovsky symphony was being played, trying to understand how so overtly emotional a composer could be of such absorbing interest to people with such a very different temperament as the Japanese. Nothing of their reaction could be read on their faces. The answer came with the burst of thunderous applause at the end of the symphony.

The tour ended glamorously, at least from my standpoint. My final appearance with the orchestra took place in Adelaide, Australia. At the request of the local concert sponsors I found myself conducting Tchaikovsky's Fifth Symphony for the first, and probably last, time. At a reception following the concert, the mayor of Adelaide, enormously impressed by the playing of the Boston Symphony, asked me to tell him frankly how his city might develop such an orchestra. Remembering what our English cousins tell Americans when they are asked how to develop a proper British lawn—"lots of rain and four hundred years"—I replied, "All you need is lots of money and seventy-five years!"

My association with the Boston Symphony, dating back to the playing of *Music for the Theatre* in 1925, took on a new dimension in 1940 with the establishment of the Berkshire Music Center. It was Serge Koussevitzky who conceived the idea of a music school for talented students as an integral part of the Orchestra's summer festival at Tanglewood. It was Koussevitzky who persuaded a somewhat reluctant board of trustees to embark on a venture that was to have important consequences for musical life in America. With the vision and enthusiasm that were characteristic of him, Koussevitzky propagandized the principle that the best students deserve the best teachers—in this instance, the leading players of the Orchestra. His own prime interest, as was natural, was the training of young conductors and of the student orchestra. But instruction in opera, choral singing, chamber music, and composition were also made an integral part of the school's activities, and there was a department for the musical amateur as well. He invited me to serve as permanent head of the Composition Department and asked Paul Hindemith to join us as guest teacher, which he did for the first two summers. For a period of twenty-five years (until my resignation in 1965), I was in contact with a cross section of America's most gifted musical youth. My summers were filled with forums, lectures, conferences, rehearsals, concerts, and composition classes. It was an exciting and a fruitful time.

It is not easy to sum up the total experience of those lively years. Three things stand out in my mind. The first is the inspired leadership of Serge Koussevitzky. Above all, it was his passionate devotion to the art of music and his deep concern for its well-being in America that communicated itself to all those who came into contact with him. A second exhilaration came from watching young talent unfold. Those of us who attended rehearsals of the student orchestra and then heard its performances under the youthful baton of fellow students such as Leonard Bernstein, Lukas Foss, Eleazar de Carvalho, and Lorin Maazel will not soon forget the special air of excitement that flashed through the Tanglewood Shed on such occasions. Finally, in more recent times, the Fromm Festival of Contemporary American Music, sponsored by the composers' friend, Paul Fromm, an enlightened music patron from Chicago, added zest and stimulus to our musical experiences by bringing to Tanglewood young creators of advanced tendencies and exceptional ability.

I plan, at some later time, to write the full story of those Tanglewood years. Not least among my pleasant memories are the weeks spent, after the close of the school term, working on my own compositions amidst the serenity of the Berkshire hills. Thus, *Quiet City* was composed in a barn studio down the road from Tanglewood after the opening season. Six years later I completed my Third Symphony in a tiny converted stable in Richmond, Massachusetts. Another barn in Richmond, with a beautiful view of open meadow and distant mountains, housed me during fourteen summers. It was there that I first consciously tried my hand at twelve-tone composition, in my Piano Quartet of 1950.

As it turned out, the Schoenberg method (not the aesthetic) continued to intrigue me in subsequent works, such as the *Piano Fantasy* (1957) and the *Connotations for Orchestra* (1962). I found twelve-tone writing to be especially liberating in two respects: it forces the tonal composer to unconventionalize his thinking with respect to chordal structure, and it tends to freshen his melodic and figurational imagination. The *Connotations* was my first twelve-tone orchestral work; it was composed on commission from the New York Philharmonic for the opening program in its new hall at Lincoln Center. The acidulous harmonies of my score, sharpened by the shrill acoustics of the new auditorium, upset a good many people, especially those who were expecting another *Appalachian Spring*. It brought to the fore once again a continuing discussion concerning the apparent dichotomy between my "serious" and my "popular" works. I can only say that those commentators who would like to split me down the middle into two opposing personalities will get no encouragement from me. I prefer to think that I write my music from a single vision; when the results differ it is because I take into account with each new piece the purpose for which it is intended and the nature of the musical materials with which I begin to work. Musical ideas engender pieces, and the ideas by their character dictate the nature of the composition to be written. It bothers me not at all to realize that my range as composer includes both accessible and problematical works. To have confined myself to a single compositional approach would have enhanced my reputation for consistency, no doubt, but would have afforded me less pleasure as a creator. The English critic Wilfrid Mellers puts it this way: "There is no fundamental disparity between the two styles; the same sensibility adapts the technique to the purpose in hand." I like to believe that what he says is true.

3. THE PRESENT DAY

The Generation of the Fifties

IT IS INTERESTING to speculate about what might have happened in the history of 20th-century music if the Second World War had not intervened. Berg had died in 1935; by the end of hostilities, Bartók and Webern were dead, and Schoenberg had passed his seventieth birthday. Stravinsky seemed committed beyond recall to a Neoclassic aesthetic, and many composers appeared happy to follow his example. Gradually, toward the end of the '40s, it became evident that a new avant-garde position was in the making. In retrospect, it is clear that fresh ideas began to take hold at the war's end: there was to some extent the same atmosphere of renewal and refreshment that I described as present at the end of the First World War: suddenly it became evident that the postwar generation of 1945 was unwilling to accept the revolution of 1920 as its own; it wanted to make its own revolution in music.

These young men of the war years had grown up during a period when Germany, France, Italy, Russia, and the Scandinavian countries were denied all access to examples of advanced composition. All such music was damned, in Nazi-occupied territories, as *Kulturbolschewismus*. The defeat of Germany ended the prohibition imposed by the Nazis. The music the members of the new generation wanted most to know was the music they had heard about and read about but had never actually experienced. The works that had been most vigorously proscribed were those of Schoenberg and his followers. But young people have a determined will to learn about precisely those things which they are told are not for them. It was out of this enforced abstinence that the impressive flood of interest in twelve-tone music was born.

The twelve-tone system has a further attraction—it is a *method;* any approach that indicates a direction and guarantees order and logic as well is in itself a great boon to the aspiring young creator.

I must admit that we of the older generation were taken by surprise. After all, the twelve-tone system was nothing new to us; in our minds it was connected almost solely with the music of Schoenberg, Berg, and Webern (though, in fact, we knew none of the later Webern works). More generally, we associated such music with Vienna and the Expressionist aesthetic, a characteristically Central European orientation. In the United States especially, the post-Romantic sensibility seemed to be not for us. What we needed was a music more optimistic in tone and more dynamic in spirit, or so it seemed then. Everything encouraged us to believe, therefore, that by 1940 the Schoenberg influence had been on the wane and that its natural stronghold in the postwar world would continue to be Central Europe. Imagine our astonishment when we discovered that the twelve-tone music of the Viennese School had become the prime interest of new composers not only in Austria and Germany, but also in France, Italy, and England, and was gradually spreading to almost all the other countries of the world.

It is true that a certain number of older composers were won over to Schoenbergian twelve-tone writing just after the war. I am thinking of men like Luigi Dallapiccola in Italy, Frank Martin in Switzerland, and Roger Sessions in the United States. But these composers would now be called moderate twelve-toners. A more radical approach to the method was soon developed by the younger generation, principally in Germany, France, and Italy, and to a more limited extent in the United States. This same younger generation discovered a more extended and unified working out of twelve-tone principles not in Schoenberg, but in Anton Webern. Before long, Schoenberg, who lived until 1951, had "the painful experience of seeing his own disciple used as a weapon against him." In the eyes of the younger men, Schoenberg was something of a backslider, if only because of his ineradicable attachment to his 19th-century past. (Let us not forget that even in his mature years in America he occasionally reverted to the writing of entirely tonal compositions.) The avant-gardists took a firm stand: they accepted Schoenberg's role as pioneer and innovator, but rejected his structural procedures and his aesthetic, looking to Webern as their newfound mentor and guide.

The postwar generation soon discovered two brilliant leaders and spokesmen—Pierre Boulez in Paris and Karlheinz Stockhausen in Cologne. Of about the same age, both had received their basic musical training in their own countries, and strangely enough, both had later been fellow students under the tutelage of Olivier Messiaen in Paris. Happily for them, they were able to write prose well, expounding their ideas in numerous and sometimes fiery polemical articles.

Boulez was particularly enterprising in propagandizing the ideas inherent in the music of Webern. In a remarkably short time he became the acknowledged head of the new musical movement in France. Through the concerts of the Domaine Musicale, an organization created and directed by Boulez, the works of the Viennese masters were heard in Paris, frequently for the first time, as were those of the new generation, many of whom were strongly Webern-oriented. A lively opposition was encountered, as was only to be expected. But Paris is ideally set up for such a situation. The small *chapelle* with new artistic ideas violently attacked by the conventional press and violently responding has been a well-known feature of French artistic life for many years.

What did Boulez and his followers wish to accomplish? This is how he himself replied to this question in a comparatively recent interview: "After the war we all felt that music, like the world around us, was in a state of chaos. Our problem was to make a new musical language, seeking out what was good from the past, and rejecting what was bad. Around 1950 and for the following three years, we went through a period of seeking out total control over music. What we were doing by total serialization was to annihilate the will of the composer in favour of a predetermining system."

The key words in this statement, it seems to me, are "total

serialization." It was not long before the term serial music was used to denote the new application of twelve-tone principles as distinguished from that of the original twelve-tone method. The difference is this: in serialism not only are the pitches under control, as in Schoenberg, but non-pitch elements, such as the rhythm, dynamics, tone color, and kinds of attack, have all been serialized as well. All parameters of a composition are under control, and each aspect of the composition is treated as a permutation of some form of the original twelve-tone row. (It is now claimed, by the way, that the American Milton Babbitt was the first composer to apply total serialization, about 1947 or 1948.)

I recall being considerably troubled when I first heard of this new theory of total control. But then, of course, one should not be overconcerned with the theories expounded by artists—it is the music they write that must hold us. One thing is certain: a great many younger composers became enamored of the idea of total serialization, and much music of very varied quality was turned out as a result. It has been sometimes referred to as "composition by numerology." Among the best new composers were Luigi Nono and Luciano Berio in Italy, Hans Werner Henze in Germany, Henri Pousseur in Belgium and Gilbert Amy and Jean-Claude Eloy in France, Witold Lutoslawski and Krzysztof Penderecki in Poland, Peter Maxwell Davies in England, and Toshiru Takemitsu and the older Matsudaira in Japan. All these men, to mention only individuals outside the Western Hemisphere, represented, in varying degrees, an avant-garde position. Not long after, a new field of application for total serialization was found in electronic music; here Stockhausen became especially active.

A typical example of serial writing is one of Boulez' chief works, *Le Marteau sans maître*. First heard in 1955, it is a setting of poems by René Char for singer and six instruments—flute, viola, guitar, vibraphone, xylorimba, and percussion. In general planning it is not unlike Schoenberg's *Pierrot lunaire*. Its instrumental coloration is more delicate—I was about to say, more French. The vocal line is obviously based on the wide leaps that have become familiar in much new music, and takes its derivation from the songs of Webern. Also typical of today's music is the incredible rhythmic and textural complexity of the work. Aside from Webern, the main influences in *Le Marteau* are Debussy, for a certain French sensitivity, and Stravinsky, for certain rhythmic procedures. It was interesting to note at the first performance, which I heard at Baden-Baden, to what an extent Boulez was able to retain characteristic French qualities, despite his serialist technique.

An ironic fact soon became evident: music under complete serialization often produced a chaotic impression on the listener. The control was entirely behind the scenes, so to speak. The music we heard seemed atomized in its texture (pointillist, it was sometimes called), and completely athematic, with no recognizable continuity of flow, and no possible way to guess what was likely to happen from one moment to the next. It naturally left a confusing impression, especially on early listeners. Many people complained that a certain static quality seemed to be an inevitable consequence of serialism. The sameness of impression, due to a lack of variety of mood and a seeming lack of personal profile, also contributed to the monotonous impression. A definite fondness for certain color schemes was evident. The overuse of glassy timbres was often remarked upon; the vibraphone, for example, soon became absolutely indispensable, as did the celesta, the harp, the glockenspiel, the piano, and other instruments of this sort. An absolute passion for percussion took hold, so that the organizers of prize competitions for new works were soon forced to announce that they could not consider entries that demanded more than seven percussion players. The new music, moreover, made extreme demands on the technical abilities of even the best interpreters. It was the experience of many good musicians that the mere reading of a strict serialist piece for their own information presented almost insuperable problems. It was as if the piece *dared* you to play it. In all, then, a strict serialism resulted usually in a music of great technical difficulty, in which the element of unpredictability was paramount. The critic Frederick Goldbeck pinpointed the unpredictable element in serialism by saying: "If the unexpected alone is allowed to happen, the moment will inevitably come when we will have to overrule the system which makes us systematically expect the unexpected."

As a matter of fact, no one overruled the system. Composers simply found that they could obtain a result, similar to that of serialization, without invoking the elaborate mystique of numbers that was inherent in complete control. The logic inherent in numbers does not guarantee a clarified impression to the listening ear; whether the composer decides to work with numbers-derived or freely choosen notes will always be secondary in importance to the music he obtains from them.

The Music of Chance

‑》》‑》》 ✦ 《‑《《‑《

THE OPPOSITE of the planned work is the work in which chance or indeterminacy plays a major role. This concept of planning for an unplanned result is, at least at present, fascinating a goodly number of composers around the world.

John Cage, born in California in 1912, is generally credited with being the inventor of chance music. As a young man he was a pupil of Henry Cowell and Schoenberg, and later he was an enthusiastic disciple of Varèse and Satie. His first "oddity" consisted in the development of the so-called prepared piano. By placing foreign objects between the strings of a piano, Cage discovered, he could transform the sound of the instrument. The piano took on a new personality—its sound became tinkly and delicately percussive, vaguely reminiscent of a Balinese gamelan orchestra.

In the early '40s Cage moved his center of activities to New York and there exerted considerable influence on a group of painters, some of whom later became famous. Gradually the composer began moving further and further away from the writing of music, pure and simple. He became an increasingly strong adherent of the philosophy of Zen, which leads to a mistrust of the rational mind and a seeking out of ways to circumvent its power over us. More and more he became intent on abdicating the artist's conscious creative power. It was with this end in view that he introduced "accidental determinants," such as the throw of dice, the toss of a coin, or the imperfections in manuscript paper, to decide the choice of notes used in his compositions. Later on, the chance events that fascinated him came to include noises of all kinds, whatever their source, either in their natural state or magnified electronically. At present Cage has practically removed himself from the sphere of music, concentrating instead on public manifestations of noise-producing phenomena for which there is no exact precedent.

How one reacts to Cage's ideas seems to me largely to depend upon one's personal temperament. Those who envisage art as a bulwark against the irrationality of man's nature, and as a monument to his constructive powers, will have no part of the Cagean aesthetic. But those who enjoy teetering on the edge of chaos will clearly be attracted. However one reacts, there is no denying that Cage's successful propagandizing of the principle of indeterminancy, not only in music but in art of all kinds, has had wide influence both here and abroad. The improvisatorial approach—with open (that is, undecided) forms, unplanned balances, and unexpected contingencies—seems likely to exert a continuing influence for some time to come.

There are, of course, different versions of the principle of indeterminancy. They range all the way from the injunction, forming the whole of one composer's "composition," to "prepare any piece and play it" to the various degrees of controlled chance introduced by some European composers. One of the first European pieces to attract attention to the aleatory idea was Karlheinz Stockhausen's *Piano Piece XI*. In this work the composer supplies the notes, which are grouped into seventeen brief sections. It is the order in which these fragments are to be played that is undetermined. Arranged on a single slab of cardboard, the entire piece is visible to the pianist at a glance. But pure chance determines where the pianist will begin, for the composer instructs him to start wherever his eyes happen to fall. Stockhausen provides various possibilities for proceeding from whatever the starting point happens to be. Thus the duration and the shape of the piece are likely to be different in successive playings. Pierre Boulez developed Cage's idea by applying it to entire movements, as in his Piano Sonata No. 3. The order in which the movements are to be played is dependent upon a decision of the executant as to where he will begin; once he has made this choice, he goes on to select among various further alternatives suggested by the composer.

The performer may either play or omit certain fragments within movements, and tempi and dynamics are subject to his whim. This wide latitude of choice practically guarantees that the work will not be played in precisely the same way in any two performances.

Other methods of assuring chance operations have been used. Some years ago the American composer Henry Brant wrote a work, *The Universal Circus*, which calls for different groups of performers, distributed in various parts of the hall, to make their contribution to the total effect by entering at previously undetermined points during the musical discourse. Thus the function of the conductor is reduced to that of a traffic cop: he leads the various groups in and out of the maze of sound without attempting to conduct the music itself. Stockhausen's orchestral work *Gruppen* is composed for equally independent groups, three moderate-sized orchestras led by three conductors. Here again unplanned simultaneities are inevitable.

It is only one step from giving the performer a limited freedom of choice to requiring that he use his own powers of musical invention by improvising his own notes. Morton Feldman, an early admirer of John Cage, has done just that in several of his compositions, including the orchestral work entitled *Out of Last Pieces*. This composition, written on graph paper, supplies no notes or rhythms for the performer.* All that is given is the number of notes to be played either chordally or in succession within the given beat, and an overall injunction concerning instrumental register (usually high) and the dynamic level (invariably soft). As might be expected, orchestral instrumentalists vary greatly in their ability to follow these instructions in an imaginative way, which can be a serious limitation in carrying out Feldman's plan.

Improvisation for smaller groups of performers has long been a familiar feature of the jazz world. Lukas Foss, working for several years with his own group of concert musicians at the University of California at Los Angeles, developed an ingenious form of group improvisation in serious music. A special feature in this

---

* Exception is made for the orchestral pianist, for whom Feldman supplies some half-dozen chords in the coda.

kind of improvising is reserved for performer reactions within the group itself——reactions which determine split-second decisions as to the shape and content of the music. In his chamber work *Echoi*, Foss specifically asks for virtuoso performers—and with reason, for the degree of random invention and strict coordination required of the performing group is truly formidable.

Earle Brown, like Feldman an associate of John Cage, posits as an ideal the creation of the work, each time anew, during its actual performance. This, he points out, is somewhat analogous to the many floating positions assumed by a Calder mobile. In the early '6os, Brown composed *Available Forms I* and *II*, for small and large orchestral groups respectively. In the latter works the composer supplies the musical events, and these are rehearsed as given; but the performances are not. What happens in an actual concert situation is described as follows by the composer: "The conductors work independently of one another but are of course dependent and related by their mutual knowledge of the combinatorial sound possibilities and by their intuitive and aural responses to the materials (events) and to each other's sound forms as they develop in the process of performing." At least one perceptive listener, Eric Salzman, describes the experience as "a kind of lively, organized, structured incoherence in which, nevertheless, a very clear relationship between the ideas and the actual form produced nearly always emerges."

As part of the unconventional approach of many younger composers to the process of composition there has developed an experimental attitude toward even the most familiar instruments, a passionate interest in exploring new performing techniques. A talented composing student of mine in Tanglewood once brought me a plan for a work for cello that consisted not of themes or musical ideas, as is customary, but of a list—a surprisingly long list—of possible ways of playing the cello. Needless to say, I learned a lot about the cello that day! (Incidentally, the student himself was not a cellist and had never before written for the cello.) With reckless disregard for what players like to play, and for the practicalities of the instruments, composers have been providing music that is, at times, playable by only a handful of specialists in contemporary music. At some point on that particular road a halt would seem inevitable.

The introduction of aleatory methods of all kinds has brought with it the necessity for inventing new kinds of musical notation. Composers of the avant garde have been more or less forced to experiment with methods for writing down their new conceptions. The result has been a babel of graphic notations, since each individual composer is a law unto himself. Pictorially many of the newly published scores are fascinating; but the question arises with each new piece, can one decipher it?

Clearly, chance as a creative principle has many varied applications. It challenges the intellect, convinced that it can produce results not otherwise obtainable. The process is amusing to contemplate; but the question remains of whether it can hold the continuing interest of a rational mind.

New Electronic Media

❊❊ ✦ ❊❊

WITH THE INTRODUCTION of electronic music a brand-new factor entered the art of music: science and scientific calculation were injected into our musical thinking.

It is a commonplace to say that we live in a scientific age. Moreover, musicians have always been aware that music and mathematics have more than a superficial relationship. After all, musical sounds can be translated into the language of numbers, and tones which we instinctively feel to be related turn out, on examination, to possess a numerical relationship. Thus, a tone is no longer merely a tone, to be accepted as a fact of nature; it can be taken apart like a mechanism and measured in frequencies, in decibels, in duration, and in kinds of attack. But that is only the beginning. The whole subject of sound waves and how they behave is under intensive investigation. Even outside the field of music, the idea of sonic exploration is familiar to the man in the street. He knows what it means to travel faster than sound, to "break the sound barrier," to use sound to detect the inner failings of machines, to study the eating habits of bats with sounds too high for the human ear to hear. In a time when the very word "sonic" is familiar to everyone, it would be strange indeed if the art of music were not profoundly affected by recent investigations.

In such circumstances, it is too much to hope that music will remain music, just as in the past. Isn't it astonishing how quickly all of us have become used to the thought that we can have a new kind of music—music without performers, without instruments, and even without composers?

These developments naturally affect the aesthetic climate within which the composer of today functions. He asks himself whether he ought not, perhaps, go back to school to study physics, acoustics, and higher mathematics, if only to save music from being taken over by the engineers and technicians. Gradually our professional musical journals begin to be filled with analyses and theories understandable only to those with adequate scientific knowledge. Unfortunately, these do not include the large majority of practicing musicians, baffled as they are by technicalities from disciplines outside their frame of reference. It is comparatively rare nowadays to read an article of musical criticism in our professional journals that concerns itself with the *human* significance of the composition under consideration. Instead, we are typically given a laboriously detailed analysis, a note-by-note and measure-by-measure dissection of considerable ingenuity, which would, in most cases, surprise the composer who wrote the piece in the first place.

What I am saying is that composers are in danger of being put out of their own house. The writing of music has begun to attract a new type of individual, half engineer and half composer. He does not approach music out of the same need as did the composer of the past; he sees it from a new perspective. To him it is an open subject with endless possibilities for experimentation, none of which need necessarily engage the subjective side of his nature. Such an investigator shares no traditional inhibitions. He has no hesitation in disposing of conventional notation if the use of other means serves his purpose better. Nor does he hesitate to apply mechanistic principles to compositional problems, the end result of which he himself cannot foretell, nor to write pieces whose virtuoso demands go far beyond the capabilities of human vocal cords and fingers.

Please do not misunderstand me. It is not my purpose to frighten the reader with ogrelike figures taken from science fiction who are about to invade the art of music. I am merely describing an important aspect of the world of creative music as it is today. Scientism has a dynamic of its own—once propelled forward, there is no way to stop it. Just as the world at large has the problem of how to absorb and incorporate the phenomenal advances of the scientific age without loss of our humanity, so the musical world must face a similar situation. Some few composers do have the training and talent needed to judge the competence of scientific minds directed to music, and these few composers can be of help at present. We must keep in mind always that musical judgment in the end belongs to the *musically* gifted, without whose sensitivity and perceptivity the whole art of music becomes an amusing game—and sometimes a not-so-amusing game.

But let us pause now to retrace our steps and outline briefly the gradual infiltration of scientific ideas into music in recent times. The composing career of Edgard Varèse may be taken as symbolic of the direction music has taken. He was one of the first composers to have had training in both scientific and musical studies. Born in France in 1883, he came to America in 1916, at the age of thirty-three, and remained in New York thereafter. Varèse had an original mind; he was never one to accept blindly traditional solutions. Although his total output is small, most of it having been composed before 1937, each work has in it some germ of the music of the future. Even the titles of his pieces are indicative: *Hyperprism, Intégrales, Arcana*—they seem to point to a more mathematical sphere of interest. And yet, at the same time, the works themselves reflect the sounds of the industrial world, using conventional instruments in a way that suggests the noises and emotional stress of modern times. In the '20s his work seemed to us limited and somewhat sectarian, but as sometimes happens, it has now taken on a larger significance. Because of the interest of the younger generation in percussion instruments and electronic sounds, Varèse's music of forty years ago has turned out to be prophetic of the new turn of events. But his own road was not an easy one. Discouraged by the lack of adequate electronic media, he gave up composing in 1937, taking it up again only in 1953, when it became possible to record sounds of all kinds on magnetic tape. In listening to his works of the '20s one may detect premonitions of the recorded sounds of today. Clearly, Varèse was a pioneer who was lucky to live long enough to see his youthful dreams take on reality.

We in the United States first became aware of the possibilities of electronic instruments when, in the early '30s, we heard concerts performed on the theremin. On this instrument only one note at a time can be played; the same limitation characterizes the instrument invented in France at about the same time, Maurice Martenot's *ondes musicales*. Not only are these two instruments monophonic by nature, but they need live performers and seem rather tricky to play. Despite the limitations, however, the Ondes Martenot enlisted the interest of French composers like Messiaen, Jolivet, and Milhaud, enjoying thereby a certain vogue.

The true breakthrough came with the invention of high-fidelity magnetic tape recorders during the Second World War. Anyone who owned one could record whatever sounds interested him. Moreover, he could edit and transform the original sounds themselves in such a way as to make them unrecognizable. The manipulation of tape in this way was first introduced in 1948 by Pierre Schaeffer, who worked with tape recorders at the Radiodiffusion Française. Under the name *musique concrète* (concrete music) the works of Schaeffer and his colleagues soon aroused considerable interest. In *musique concrète* the experiments were confined to the manipulation of "natural" sounds such as those of a bell, a gong, or dripping water. An interesting parallel has been made between *musique concrète* and the art of the cinema. Both media work with concrete images in a certain rhythm, within the framework of a scenario or schema. Thus, the composer of *musique concrète* takes as his point of departure *"objets sonores* which are the equivalent of visual images, and which therefore alter the procedures of musical composition completely." The natural affinity of *musique concrète* for theatrical forms such as television, movies, ballet, and drama is obvious.

By 1954 a new conception of tape music had emerged from the official German broadcasting studio in Cologne. Here the experimenters preferred to deny themselves the realistically derived sounds of *musique concrète,* concentrating on synthetic sounds produced by various types of tone generators. Suddenly avant-garde composers found themselves deeply involved with electronics, delving into a new world of seemingly endless possibilities. Electronic music, as it came to be called, was fortunate in gaining the interest and cooperation of experienced composers such as Stockhausen, Krenek, Varèse, and Boulez. Before long other centers of electronic experimentation were developed in Milan, Amsterdam, New York, and Tokyo—to name only a few. In the last few years many of the music departments of North American universities have inaugurated their own electronic studios.

It is easy to understand the fascination for composers of this new medium. A composer colleague once taped one tiny sound for me—a "boom," in pianissimo. I was astonished at the variety of effects that could transform this tiny noise all the way from a faint whisper to a roaring waterfall. Through varying the frequency and amplitude of the original, through reverberation, speed control, montage, and so forth, new vistas are opened up. Other advantages were immediately apparent. The electronic generator does away with many of the limitations of conventional music, starting with the half-tone divisions of the scale; it adds chordal structures of unprecedented complexity, produces unheard-of gradations of loud and soft, and dispenses with the need for live performers.

But there are disadvantages also. The basic sine tones produced by the generator have little tonal variety; consequently much tape music has a depressing sameness of sound. Moreover, the fact that each new composition has to be laboriously built up, sound by sound, with nothing "given," makes the composing process painfully slow. A few minutes of such music may take several weeks to prepare. But even more serious is the built-in monotony which results because the performance, being on tape, is always precisely the same. Each repetition makes one yearn for the unpredictability of live performers. Some means have been found to overcome in part these two drawbacks. To avoid monotony, electronic composers soon began writing works for tape *and* live performers. Thus one could have the human touch, certain to add differences with each performance. Otto Luening and Vladimir Ussachevsky, two United States composers, were among the first to write for combinations of normal orchestra and taped sounds. Speed in writing was greatly increased by the invention, at the RCA Princeton acoustic laboratories, of an electronic music synthesizer. According to Milton Babbitt, professor of music at Princeton, who has been given the "care and feeding" of this machine, the synthesizer can do anything, and do it faster. The principal drawback is that the synthesizer is a rare instrument; the only one now in existence cost about $150,000.

In 1959 appeared *Experimental Music*, a book written jointly by a mathematician and a music professor at the University of Illinois, L. M. Isaacson and L. A. Hiller. This book had the disturbing subtitle: *Composition with an Electronic Computer.* It opened the door to a whole new wonderworld of automation—a world in which the computer is made to outdo the composer's brain, provided, of course, that the proper information is supplied the machine in the first place. In one of the earliest forms of this new venture, the most frequent characteristics of melodic writing were analyzed, coded, and fed into the computer, and it was shown that an endless number of simple but quite well-proportioned melodies might be composed by the machine itself. Clearly we have here arrived at the end of the line which began with no microphones, no instruments, no performers—now there are no composers. The coauthors of the book tell us that they composed, with the help of the computer, a four-movement string quartet which, though they modestly do not claim it to be a work of art, they definitely describe as *musica ex machina*. More important, they foresee a time when computers will aid contemporary composers in changing and extending compositional techniques. In addition, computers may lead us to "radically different species of music based upon fundamentally new techniques of musical analysis." All this appears logical to me, since automation was developed in order to outthink the human brain in other areas, and its application to music must be only a matter of time. At present, computers have been invented which not only create the notes but also perform them. Surely it is only a short step from machines which perform to machines capable of writing out scores and parts in normal notation for composers of noncomputer music. What a saving in time and expense!

It is clear from this brief outline that tape music of different kinds is likely to influence music of the future. It has the great advantage of novelty. Also, it is well designed for being sent through the mails and for subsequent dissemination by means of broadcasting facilities throughout the world. Already many millions of people 'are familiar with the sound of electronic music through its use as background accompaniment for films.

The reader may be wondering what I, as a composer, think of the electronic music of our time. My primary concern is to prevent myself from coming too quickly to conclusions. This is not timidity or fear of being wrong. It is rather a realistic approach. After all, electronic and computer music are hardly ten years old. The media are brand new, with many years of experimentation ahead—why then is it necessary for us to be in such a hurry to make up our minds about their artistic value? My attitude therefore is permissive, giving the new composers the benefit of the doubt. I am a great believer in the salutary effects of error; by making mistakes we find the right way. There is no doubt that a veritable Pandora's box of new musical possibilities has overwhelmed the present generation of composers. But it is useless to attempt to shut the box and turn our heads. I agree with the American physics professor John Backus when he writes: "The proper application of the methods and results of scientific investigation can be of tremendous benefit to the field of music. This does not mean that music will be taken over by science; the scientic method has its limitations, and its proper application includes not only the recognition of these limits but also the obligation to expose any misapplication of scientific method and terminology to music, since it is equally obvious that such misapplication can do a great deal of damage."

All past musical history shows us that our art cannot remain static. Whether it is moving forward well or badly can only be determined from a greater perspective than we now have. Fortunately there is no one way to which we are committed. With open minds and a good amount of forbearance the musical challenges of the future will have to be met. As Marc Wilkinson has written: "We have inherited new worlds, and part of our work is to chart these, to explore and cultivate them, and to grow new fruit."

Index

✦